Cook
Bookles
4/22

Cakes, Cookies and Pastries

Cakes, Cookies and Pastries

MYRA WALDO

GALAHAD BOOKS • NEW YORK CITY

Contents

Introduction
  Thoughts About Making Cakes, Cookies and Pastry   7

Cakes   17

Tortes   49

Cookies   58

Macaroons   69

Pie   78

Pastry   92

Tarts   104

Quick Section—Cakes and Pies Prepared with Mixes   110

Frostings, Creams, Glazes and Fillings   114

Conversion Chart   121

Index   123

Introduction

Thoughts About Making Cakes, Cookies and Pastry

THE ABILITY to make fine cakes, cookies and pastry is the hall-mark of the accomplished cook. Learning to bake is no longer surrounded by mystery, for over the years, science has ana-lyzed the reasons for success (and failure) in baking. By fol-lowing a set of rules, it is possible to have success in all cake-making endeavors. But the essential is that these rules be followed.

It is only in cake-making that the cook is strictly limited to the wording of the recipe. In preparing a meat casserole, for example, the cook is at liberty to add her own little touches, such as adding carrots even when the recipe does not call for them. If a recipe specifies beef broth and an unusually enterprising cook uses white wine instead, the result will of course be quite different, but not necessarily disastrous. In some cases, the cook may even use a different meat than the one called for in making a casserole, such as veal in place of beef. The finished dish may taste quite different from the one described in the recipe, and it may turn out to be good or not quite so good. But the finished casserole will be edible, in any event.

This is not true of cakes or pastry. Small variations in a recipe, even those that might seem only a matter of personal taste or creative expression, could easily result in a poor cake, sometimes even a downright inedible failure. It is impossible to get successful results if the recipe is merely used as a start-ing point or springboard for a freewheeling expression of the cook's personality, as is commonly done in making appetizers, soups, fish, meats or salads. As with all recipes, but particu-larly those for cakes or pastry, you should read the recipe through *first*, before you do anything. It is very disconcerting to find, in the middle of making a cake, that there is no baking powder in the kitchen, for example, and substitutions are never completely satisfactory. It is always advisable to check your ingredients before taking even the first step. Cake recipes are a matter of checks and balances, of using just the right amount of leavening in proportion to eggs and flour, of the right amount of shortening in proportion to the dry ingredients. If one of these factors were to be altered, the result would probably be disappointing.

The author receives hundreds of letters each year asking why certain cakes succeed and others fail. An analysis of the complaints in these letters suggests that in ninety per cent (or more) of the cases, the difficulty lies in either reading the recipe incorrectly or in not following the instructions carefully. In the remaining cases, the trouble arises from a variety of sources, such as improperly regulated ovens, stale ingredients, ingredients combined at the wrong temperature, egg whites beaten when ice cold, and so on. But the greatest single cause of difficuty seems to stem simply from a failure to follow the recipes closely and without variation.

A cake can only be as good as the ingredients that go into it. Needless to say, truly fresh butter will make a better cake than butter which has been in the refrigerator for weeks, gradually losing its flavor; and of course, creamery butter makes a better product than does margarine. If baking powder is called for, and you use an opened can of year-old baking powder, you can expect much of its lifting qualities to be gone. A package of flour that has been left open will absorb moisture from the air on humid days and will often make a heavy, streaky cake. It is essential that all baking ingredients, such as flour or baking powder, be stored in a tightly covered container and kept away from air.

How to Become a Good Baker

1. Read the recipe over at least twice, slowly and carefully.

2. If you have any doubts about the meaning of the terms used in the recipe, look them up in the section on definitions beginning on page 00.

3. If the recipe calls for eggs, remove them from the refrigerator at least one hour before using, so that they can come up to room temperature. If they are to be separated, separate them immediately upon taking them from the refrigerator.

4. Arrange in a convenient place *all* of the ingredients called for in the cake.

5. Make sure that the pan you intend to use is the correct size; this is quite important, for an outsized pan would result in a flat cake, with a texture, appearance and taste totally different from what you anticipated. A small pan would result in an overexpanded cake, which would also be unsatisfactory. Use only shiny, unspotted pans for cakes, for they reflect heat best. Pies may be baked in glass pie plates.

6. Preheat the oven at least 20 minutes in advance, so that the oven can come up to the proper temperature. Oven temperatures must be checked carefully, for thermostats frequently go out of order. Place a small oven thermometer (they may be purchased for about $1) in the oven to check the thermostat from time to time.

7. In recipes, standardized measures are used, including teaspoons, tablespoons and cups. This does not mean that you may use any handy teaspoon, tablespoon or cup in your kitchen. One ordinary household tablespoon may hold twice as much as another tablespoon; it is *absolutely essential* that the standard measuring teaspoon, tablespoon and cup be used. If not, the entire balance of ingredients will be lost, and disappointment will inevitably follow.

8. Which rack in the oven should you use? Where there are no special instructions, place the cake on a rack in the middle of the oven, centering the cake as much as possible, so that heated air can circulate evenly around the cake. Don't put anything else in the oven when making a cake, for this will interfere with proper baking. It would be poor economy to bake two large cakes at the same time, only to find that neither is properly baked. However, shallow cakes may be baked a few at a time if the recipe specifically calls for it. Assuming that the average oven has two racks, dividing the oven into three levels, you should follow these general rules:

Bottom: Never use this for baking, for the bottom of the cake would be overly browned with the top remaining partially unbaked.

Middle: This is best for almost all baking, particularly unfilled pie or pastry shells.

Top: This should be used only to brown quickly, or caramelize, the tops of cakes. Ordinarily, baking on the top rack would produce cakes which are too brown on top and unbaked on the bottom.

9. The baking time specified in each recipe can only be approximate because of the many variables (freshness of leavening, temperature variations in ovens, amount of kneading, etc.). It is quite essential that cakes be tested shortly before the end of the baking time specified. This is done best with a "cake tester" or a long toothpick or wooden match. If dough adheres to the cake tester or toothpick, the cake is not done. The tester should come out "clean," or almost dry. Another test is to press the cake gently with your finger; the cake should spring back quickly. If your finger leaves an impression on the surface, the cake is not done.

10. The recipes in this book are best suited for altitudes from sea level to 3,000 feet. If you live at a higher altitude, you will have to make a few allowances. First, because flour becomes drier and more compact at high altitudes, you should use slightly less of it than the recipe calls for. Second, you should use yeast somewhat sparingly since yeast action is stronger at high altitudes. Third, you should increase your baking temperature very slightly: for example, if the recipe calls for 350°, make it 360°. However, high-altitude baking varies somewhat from recipe to recipe, and only by experimenting will you find the correct allowances for a given cake or pastry.

11. To cool the cake, place the pan on a cake rack, so that air can circulate on all sides; if the cake is placed on a counter or other solid surface, no air can circulate under the bottom of the cake, and it will cool unevenly, with undesirable results. Unless otherwise directed, let the cake cool for about 15 minutes, then loosen the sides gently from the pan with a spatula. Then remove the cake rack from under the cake pan, and place the rack on top of the pan. Invert quickly, holding

cake rack and cake pan together, remove the pan, and let the cake cool further.

Definitions of Baking Terms

Bake: Cook in a heated oven.

Beat: Incorporate air into ingredients. When the ingredients are soft (like egg whites), this is best done by means of an electric mixer, a rotary beater or a wire whisk. When the ingredients are firm (like a batter), the beating is best done with an electric mixer or with a wooden spoon.

Blend: Mix together two or more ingredients until combined.

Chill: Place in a refrigerator until cold to the touch.

Cream: Soften butter (or other shortening); it may be done with a kitchen spoon or by electric mixer. Sometimes two or more ingredients are creamed together, that is, softened and mixed together at the same time.

Cut in shortening: Use two knives (or a special kitchen tool called a "pastry blender") in a crisscross fashion to cut the shortening so that it combines with the flour, in that way causing the formation of flour-covered particles of fat. Hands cannot be used because their natural body warmth would interfere with the process.

Dot: Place small bits of an ingredient (usually butter) on the surface of the cake being prepared.

Fold in: Incorporate air into a mixture while combining the ingredients. This process is extremely important, for if air is not incorporated into the mixture, the cake will not rise properly. The process: First (in the absence of other, specific instructions), put the batter in a fairly large bowl. Next, pile the beaten egg whites lightly on top of the batter. Use a wire whisk, a large spoon or a spatula, and *very gently and slowly* bring the whisk (or spoon or spatula) downward into the mixture and then upward to make a complete circular motion. As you do this, some of the batter will be lifted out onto the egg whites, and on the downward motion some of the egg whites will be mixed into the batter. Continue this until the ingredients are reasonably well mixed together: the egg whites need not be completely combined with the batter; some patches of egg whites may be visible. It is important, however, that the folding process be done slowly and gently.

Grease: Spread butter, margarine or oil on a surface, such as a cooky sheet, muffin cup, etc.

Knead: Handle dough to bring it to a desired consistency. If the dough has some firmness or consistency to begin with, it is best kneaded on a board, although any flat surface will do. Lightly sprinkle flour on the surface. Flour the hands lightly, then flatten the dough just a little and shape into a ball. (The dough will be somewhat flat on top.) Fold the dough in half, and using the heel of the hand, press down and away from you then, fold over again and press down again. Each time, turn the dough to the left, so that you are always kneading a different part of the dough. Keep this up until the dough is elastic, smooth, and satiny. This should take from 8 to 10 minutes. It may be necessary to use a bit more flour on the surface or on the hands when the dough becomes sticky. If the unkneaded dough is very soft or sticky, it may be advisable to knead the dough in a bowl.

Preheat: Allow the oven temperature to reach a desired degree of heat in advance; this usually requires about 20 minutes.

Roll out dough: Form and thin the dough. If the dough has been refrigerated, remove 10 minutes before using to allow it to soften a little; however, it cannot remain at room temperature much longer than 10 minutes or the dough will become soft and tacky and difficult to work with. Form the dough by hand into a rectangle, or any other desired shape. Dough may be rolled on any large flat surface, although a piece of marble is probably the best. A table top or a pastry cloth may also be used, in which case a very small amount of flour should first be sprinkled on the flat surface and also on the rolling pin. (Another technique is to roll dough out between two sheets of waxed paper, in which case no flour need be used.) Roll out fairly lightly *in one direction only*—away from you. Lift up the rolling pin and roll again. After every few rolls, turn the dough a quarter turn so that the longer dimension of the rolled dough now extends from left to right. Continue rolling until the dough is the proper thinness. Use as little flour as possible, although a small additional amount may be required to keep the dough from sticking to the board or to the rolling pin. It is not necessary to press down very hard to roll dough properly unless the dough is too cold.

Scald: Heat liquids to just below the boiling point. In scalding, a typical formation of bubbles appears around the outside edges but not in the middle of the saucepan.

Stir: Mix together ingredients until well-blended, using a spoon. Do not stir too long. You should stop just as soon as the ingredients are combined.

Whip: Beat speedily, usually cream or egg whites, to add air and increase the volume of the ingredients.

Baking Ingredients

Flour: There are many different kinds of flour on the market, and this profusion might call for a degree of caution among cake-makers. Standard flour, called "all-purpose," may in general be used for any recipe in this book, unless otherwise specified. However, it does result in a somewhat more coarsely textured cake than "cake flour" would, the latter being made from a soft variety of winter wheat. The difference, though, is not particularly discernible when cakes are made with eggs; in this case, all-purpose flour is often satisfactory. Self-rising flours are those which already contain baking powder and salt; they are not generally recommended, but if you use them, omit the leavening and salt from the recipe.

Flour should be sifted before using, even though the flour is labeled "pre-sifted," because as moisture accumulates, the flour loses some of its packaged (original) qualities.

Sift all flour first, then measure.

Baking powder: All recipes in this book require the type of baking called "double-acting," which means that the baking powder has two rising actions. The first takes place when the powder is mixed with a liquid, causing a partial formation of gas; the second rising occurs when the batter is heated, causing the gas to expand and resulting in a more evenly leavened product.

Shortening: Butter makes the best cakes, but margarine may be used with results that are almost as good. The hydrogenated (solid) shortenings may be used, but flavor changes may be expected, for these hydrogenated shortenings are flavorless. Salad oil may be used whenever melted shortening is called for, but the results may be somewhat indifferent. Lard has a strong flavor, and bakers unfamiliar with its taste might do well to avoid its use in cakes. Lard can be used for pie pastry, however. All in all, there can be no doubt that butter or margarine is the best shortening for making fine cakes and pastry.

Eggs: There is little or no difference between brown and white eggs. If the recipe calls for eggs, see that they are fresh; stale eggs tend to deteriorate, causing a lessening of flavor and therefore a poorer taste in the finished cake. Refrigerate eggs until you are ready to use them; if the recipe calls for separated eggs, separate them immediately upon removal from the refrigerator. Then allow them to stand at room temperature for 1 hour before using. Egg whites will beat up properly only at room temperature, but eggs separate best when cold. When whole eggs are added to a recipe, add them one at a time, unless instructions call for prebeating.

What size egg should you use in a recipe? Obviously, all eggs vary slightly in size, but average, medium-sized eggs are the kind suggested for these recipes. However, if the available eggs are very small, use 3 small eggs for every 2 specified in the recipe. A reverse adjustment may be made if only very large (jumbo) eggs are available.

Sugar: White sugar should be sifted before use. Fine granulated sugar must be used, or the cake will have a somewhat coarse texture. Brown sugar, naturally lumpy and sticky, must be measured carefully. It should be packed into a measuring cup so firmly that it will hold together when removed.

Chocolate: Because chocolate has a low burning point, it should always be heated over indirect heat, never over direct heat. Do not add melted chocolate directly to other ingredients after removing it from the heat; allow it to cool for a minute or two.

How to Check the Cause of Cake Failure

Cake falls
1. Flour may be stale, or incorrectly measured.
2. Cake did not bake long enough, or oven was opened before center was firmly set.
3. Oven temperature out of regulation.

Cake is flat and insufficiently risen
1. Pan used was too large for amount of batter.
2. Not enough leavening, or leavening was stale.
3. Wrong oven temperature.

Cake has a coarse-grained texture
1. All-purpose flour used; use cake flour.
2. Check carefully the measurements of all ingredients; possible error in proportions of ingredients used.
3. Excess leavening or too many egg yolks.
4. Oven temperature too low.
5. Ingredients not mixed together smoothly enough.
6. Sugar not fine enough.

Cake is too soft and falls apart
1. Excessive sugar, leavening, shortening; check measurements.
2. Not enough eggs, or stale eggs.
3. Oven temperature too low; or cake removed from pan before cooled.

Cake pulls away from sides of cakepan
1. Ingredients not at room temperature when combined. (This is particularly important for egg whites and liquids which should be at room temperature, not cold.)
2. Ingredients improperly mixed together.
3. Too much liquid used; check measurements of ingredients.

4. Oven temperature wrong; probably baked too long for temperature used.
5. Insufficient amount of batter for size of pan; measure size of pans.

Cake is too heavy
1. Excessive amounts of sugar, flour or fat; check amount specified against amount used.
2. Oven temperature wrong—probably too hot.
3. Too much mixing of batter; air bubbles may have broken down in overmixing.
4. If eggs whites used, may not have been gently combined with other ingredients.

Cakes

VIENNESE CHOCOLATE LAYER CAKE

1¾ cups sifted cake flour
1 teaspoon salt
2 teaspoons baking powder
1½ cups sugar
½ cup butter or margarine
1¼ cups light cream

2 eggs
1 teaspoon vanilla extract
2 squares (ounces)
    unsweetened chocolate,
    melted and cooled

Preheat oven to 350°. Grease two 9-inch layer cake pans and dust lightly with a little flour.

Sift together the flour, salt, baking powder and sugar. Cream the butter; sift in the flour mixture. Mix in 1 cup cream, then beat very well. Add the eggs, vanilla, chocolate and remaining cream. Beat very well again. Divide batter evenly between the two prepared pans. Bake 25 minutes or until a cake tester comes out clean. Cool on a cake rack 10 minutes before removing from pans. Cool thoroughly before frosting with rich Chocolate Frosting (see recipe).

RICH CHOCOLATE CAKE, ARGENTINE STYLE

2½ cups sifted cake flour
½ teaspoon salt
1 teaspoon baking soda
¼ pound sweet chocolate
½ cup brewed coffee
1 cup (2 sticks) butter

1¾ cups sugar
4 egg yolks
1 cup buttermilk or sour
    milk
4 egg whites, stiffly beaten

Preheat oven to 350°. Grease three 8-inch layer cake pans and dust lightly with flour.

Sift together the flour, salt and baking soda. Combine the chocolate and coffee in the top of a double boiler; place over hot water until melted. Cool. Cream the butter; gradually beat in the sugar until light and fluffy. Add 1 egg yolk at a time, beating well after each addition. Mix in the melted chocolate. Add the flour mixture alternately with the buttermilk, beating until smooth after each adition. Fold in the egg whites. Divide bater evenly among the prepared pans. Bake 35 minutes or until a cake tester comes out clean. Cool on a cake rack 20 minutes before removing from pans. Cool thoroughly before frosting with Seven Minute Frosting, Cream Frosting or Whipped Cream.

Note: This cake is very rich and may crack and fall, but the flavor won't be affected.

DANISH CHOCOLATE YEAST CAKE

2 *envelopes yeast*
¼ *cup warm water*
¾ *cup milk, scalded and cooled*
3 *cups sifted flour*
½ *cup (1 stick) butter*
2 *cups sugar*

3 *eggs*
1 *package semi-sweet chocolate morsels, melted*
1 *teaspoon baking soda*
½ *teaspoon salt*
½ *teaspoon vanilla extract*

Sprinkle the yeast into the water and stir until dissolved. Beat in the milk and 1½ cups flour until smooth. Cover and let rise in a warm place until light and spongy, about 30 minutes.

Meanwhile, cream together the butter and sugar. Add 1 egg at a time, beating well after each addition. Add yeast mixture, remaining flour, melted chocolate, baking soda, salt and vanilla. Beat until well-blended. Turn into a well-greased 10-inch tube pan. Cover and let rise in a warm place, free from draft, until light and bubbly, about 1 hour. Bake in a preheated 350° oven 50 minutes, or until a cake tester inserted in center comes out clean. Cool on a cake rack 15 minutes, then turn out onto the rack. Let stand until cold. Serve with Coffee Whipped Cream or split the cake into three layers and fill with the flavored whipped cream.

UPSIDE-DOWN CHOCOLATE CAKE

1 cup sifted flour
¼ teaspoon salt
2 teaspoons baking powder
1¼ cups granulated sugar
7 tablespoons unsweetened
  cocoa
¾ cup milk
1 teaspoon vanilla extract

2 tablespoons melted butter
  or margarine
½ cup chopped walnuts or
  pecans
½ cup firmly packed brown
  sugar
1 cup water

Preheat oven to 350°. Grease an 8-inch square baking pan.
Sift the flour, salt, baking powder, ¾ cup granulated sugar
and 2 tablespoons cocoa into a bowl. Mix in the milk and
vanilla until smooth. Stir in the melted butter and nuts lightly.
Spread evenly in the prepared pan. In a saucepan mix the
brown sugar, water, remaining granulated sugar and cocoa.
Bring to a boil, stirring until sugars dissolve. Pour over the
batter in the pan. Bake 40 minutes, or until a cake tester
comes out clean. Cool on a cake rack 20 minutes, then turn
out, bottom up. The fudge will now be on top. Cool and cut
into 2-inch squares.

CHOCOLATE CHIFFON CAKE

1¾ cups sifted cake flour
1 teaspoon baking soda
2½ teaspoons cream of tartar
2 cups sugar
⅔ cup unsweetened cocoa
½ cup vegetable oil

7 egg yolks
¾ cup cold water
1 teaspoon vanilla extract
1 cup egg white (9-10)
1 teaspoon salt

Preheat oven to 350°.
Sift together the flour, baking soda, 2 teaspoons cream of
tartar, the sugar and cocoa into a large bowl. Make a well in
the center and in it put the oil, egg yolks, water and vanilla.
Beat until thoroughly blended.
Beat together the egg whites, salt and remaining cream of
tartar until very stiff. Fold into the chocolate mixture care-

fully but thoroughly. Pour into a 10-inch tube pan. Bake 1 hour and 10 minutes or until a cake tester comes out clean. Invert and let cool in the pan (upside down) for 2 hours. (If tube pan doesn't have legs to keep top of cake away from a rack, put the center part in a bottle. Air must circulate.) Run a spatula around the edges and center tube, then turn out.

FUDGE CAKE

3 cups sifted cake flour	*1¾ cups milk*
½ teaspoon salt	*2¼ cups sugar*
1½ teaspoons baking soda	*¾ cup shortening*
5 eggs	*1½ teaspoons vanilla extract*
4 squares (ounces)	
unsweetened chocolate	

Preheat oven to 350°. Grease three 9-inch layer cake pans and dust lightly with flour.

Sift together the flour, salt and baking soda. In a saucepan, beat 1 egg. Add the chocolate, broken into small pieces, ¾ cup milk and 1 cup sugar. Cook over low heat, stirring constantly, until chocolate melts. Cool.

Cream the shortening; gradually beat in the remaining sugar until light and fluffy. Add 1 of the remaining eggs at a time, beating after each addition. Add the flour mixture alternately with the remaining milk, beating well after each addition. Blend in the vanilla and chocolate mixture. Divide batter evenly among the prepared pans. Bake 30 minutes or until a cake tester comes out clean. Cool on a cake rack 20 minutes before removing from pans. Cool thoroughly before frosting.

CHEESECAKE WITH SOUR CREAM

1 cup graham cracker crumbs	*¼ cup sifted flour*
½ cup ground almonds	*5 egg yolks*
¼ cup melted butter	*2 tablespoons lemon juice*
1½ pounds cream cheese,	*1 teaspoon vanilla extract*
at room temperature	*½ teaspoon almond extract*
1¼ cups sugar	*1 cup sour cream*
1 teaspoon salt	*5 egg whites*

Mix together the crumbs, nuts and melted butter. Pack onto the bottom of a greased 10-inch spring form. Chill 30 minutes.

Beat together the cheese, 1 cup sugar and the salt. Add the flour and 1 egg yolk at a time, beating until very smooth. Beat in the lemon juice, vanilla, almond extract and sour cream.

Beat the egg whites until soft peaks form, then gradually beat in the remaining sugar until stiff but not dry; fold into the cheese mixture. Slowly pour into the prepared chilled spring-form. Bake in a preheated 325° oven 1¼ hours. Open the oven door and leave cake to cool for 1 hour. Remove from oven and finish cooling on a cake rack, then chill before removing the sides of the pan.

Serves 10–12.

COCONUT CHEESECAKE

1 pound cream cheese, at
   room temperature
¾ cup sugar
4 egg yolks
2 tablespoons flour
½ teaspoon salt

¼ cup fine-grated coconut
⅔ cup heavy cream
1 tablespoon cognac
4 egg whites
1 9-inch pastry or coconut
   shell

Preheat oven to 325°.

Beat the cream cheese until smooth, then beat in ½ cup sugar gradually. Add 1 egg yolk at a time, beating after each addition. Stir in the flour, salt and coconut, then the cream and cognac.

Beat the egg whites until stiff; gradually beat in the remaining ¼ cup sugar. Fold into the cheese mixture. Pour into the lined pie plate. Bake 45 minutes or until a knife inserted in the center comes out clean. Open the door and let cake cool in the oven 1 hour. Remove from oven to finish cooling.

REFRIGERATOR CHEESECAKE

18 zwieback, finely crushed
¼ pound (1 stick) butter, melted
¾ cup sugar
2 envelopes (tablespoons) gelatin
½ cup water
1 pound cream cheese

3 egg yolks
½ cup light cream
2 teaspoons grated lemon rind
1 tablespoon lemon juice
½ teaspoon salt
1 cup whipped cream
3 egg whites, stiffly beaten

Combine the zwieback, melted butter and ¼ cup sugar. Press on the bottom and sides of a 9-inch buttered spring form.

Soften the gelatin in the water for 5 minutes. Place over hot water and stir until dissolved.

Beat the remaining sugar and cheese; add the egg yolks, light cream, lemon rind, lemon juice, salt and gelatin. Beat until light and fluffy.

Fold the whipped cream into the cheese mixture. Fold the egg whites in carefully but thoroughly. Pour into the prepared spring form. Chill at least 4 hours.

SPICE SOUR CREAM CAKE

2 cups sifted flour
¼ teaspoon salt
1 teaspoon baking soda
2 teaspoons cinnamon
1 teaspoon ground allspice
½ teaspoon ground cloves

¼ pound (1 stick) butter
2 cups packed dark brown sugar
3 eggs
1 cup sour cream

Preheat oven to 350°. Grease two 9-inch layer cake pans.

Sift together the flour, salt, baking soda, cinnamon, allspice and cloves. Cream the butter; gradually beat in the brown sugar until light and fluffy. Add 1 egg at a time, beating well after each addition. Add the sifted ingredients alternately with the sour cream, mixing only until blended. Turn into the pans.

Bake 30 minutes or until a cake tester comes out clean. Cool on a cake rack 10 minutes, then turn out and cool completely before putting together with Butter Cream or whipped cream.

ITALIAN SPICE NUT CAKE

(CERTOSINA)

1 cup sifted flour
¼ teaspoon salt
½ teaspoon baking soda
½ teaspoon ground cloves
½ teaspoon nutmeg
½ teaspoon cinnamon
½ cup sugar

½ cup honey
⅔ cup water
2½ cups blanched toasted sliced almonds
½ cup finely diced candied fruits

Sift together the flour, salt, baking soda, cloves, nutmeg and cinnamon.

Combine the sugar, honey and water in a saucepan. Cook over low heat, stirring constantly, until mixture boils. Remove from the heat and beat in the flour mixture until very smooth. Mix in the almonds and fruit. Turn into a well-oiled 9-inch pie plate. If you like, decorate the top with almonds and fruit. Bake in a preheated 300° oven 45 minutes or until a cake tester comes out clean. Cool thoroughly before turning out. Serve in very narrow strips.

BRAZILIAN NUT CAKE

10 egg yolks
1 teaspoon instant coffee
1¾ cups superfine sugar
3 cups ground nuts (walnuts, brazil, almonds)

⅛ teaspoon salt
2 tablespoons cognac
2 tablespoons bread crumbs
10 egg whites

Butter a 10-inch spring form and dust lightly with bread crumbs.

Beat the egg yolks and instant coffee; gradually add the

sugar, beating until thick and light. Mix in the ground nuts, salt, cognac and the 2 tablespoons bread crumbs. Beat the egg whites until stiff but not dry; fold into the nut mixture. Turn into the prepared pan. Bake in a preheated 350° oven 50 minutes, or until a cake tester comes out clean. Cool on a cake rack before removing the pan. Split and fill and cover with coffee-flavored whipped cream, if you like.

BRAZILIAN CHOCOLATE NUT CAKE

2¾ cups sifted cake flour
½ teaspoon salt
2 teaspoons baking powder
¼ pound sweet chocolate
¼ cup brewed coffee
1 cup (2 sticks) butter
1½ cups sugar

4 egg yolks
1 teaspoon vanilla extract
¾ cup milk
1 cup finely chopped filberts,
   walnuts or pecans
4 egg whites

Preheat oven to 350°. Grease a 10-inch tube pan and dust lightly with flour.

Sift together the flour, salt and baking powder. Break the chocolate into small pieces and combine with the coffee in the top of a double boiler. Place over hot water until melted; cool.

Cream the butter. Gradually beat in the sugar until light and fluffy. Add 1 egg yolk at a time, beating well after each addition. Blend in the vanilla and melted chocolate. Add the flour mixture alternately with the milk, beating until smooth after each addition. Stir in the nuts. Beat the egg whites until stiff but not dry; fold into the chocolate mixture. Pour into the prepared pan; smooth the top with a spatula. Bake 1 hour or until a cake tester comes out clean. Cool on a cake rack 20 minutes before removing from pan. The cake may be served as is, cut in wedges, or split into as many layers as you like. Whipped cream or any filling may then be spread between the layers.

SPONGE CAKE

6 egg whites	1 tablespoon lemon juice
⅛ teaspoon salt	1 teaspoon vanilla extract
1⅛ cups fine granulated sugar	1 teaspoon grated lemon rind
6 egg yolks	1 cup sifted flour

Preheat oven to 350°. Grease only the bottom of a 9-inch tube pan and dust it lightly with flour.

Beat the egg whites and salt until soft peaks form, then beat in 1 tablespoon of sugar at a time, beating steadily until stiff.

Beat the egg yolks until thick, then mix in the lemon juice, vanilla and rind. Fold about 1 cup of the egg whites into the yolks until no white remains. Pile the remaining egg whites on the yolk mixture, then sift flour over them. Fold together carefully. Turn into the pan and smooth top with a rubber scraper. Pick up pan carefully and hit bottom on a hard surface.

Bake 40 minutes or until top springs back when pressed with the finger and is browned. Cool on a cake rack.

Note: For layers, bake in two 9-inch layer cake pans for 25 minutes or until done.

ORANGE SPONGE CAKE

4 egg yolks	1¼ cups sifted cake flour
¾ cup sugar	4 egg whites
⅓ cup orange juice	⅛ teaspoon salt
2 teaspoons grated orange rind	

Preheat oven to 350°. Place oven rack on middle level. Grease a 9-inch layer cake pan and dust lightly with flour.

Beat the egg yolks, then gradually add the sugar (reserving 2 tablespoons) beating with an electric mixer or wire whisk until thick and light. Beat in the orange juice and rind, then mix in the flour.

Beat the egg whites and salt until soft peaks are formed, then beat in the reserved sugar until stiff but not dry. Fold half the egg whites into the flour mixture then fold in the remaining egg whites lightly. Turn into the pan. Bake 30 minutes or until browned and slightly shrunk away from the sides of the pan. Cool in the pan 5 minutes, then run a spatula around the edge and turn out onto a cake rack. Turn right side up and let stand until cold. Sprinkle with powdered sugar or split, fill with Orange Cream Filling and glaze with Orange Glaze.

ALMOND-COGNAC SPONGE CAKE

3 egg yolks
¾ cup sugar
⅓ cup cognac
¼ teaspoon almond extract
¾ cup ground blanched
    almonds

¾ cup sifted cake flour
¼ pound (1 stick) butter,
    melted and cooled
3 egg whites
⅛ teaspoon salt

Preheat oven to 350°. Place oven rack on middle level. Grease a 9-inch layer cake pan and dust lightly with flour.

Beat the egg yolks with an electric mixer or wire whisk; gradually add the sugar (reserving 2 tablespoons) beating until thick and light. Beat in the cognac and almond extract. Mix in the almonds and flour. Fold in the butter.

Beat the egg whites and salt until soft peaks are formed. Beat in the reserved sugar until stiff but not dry. Fold half the egg whites into the almond mixture, then fold in the remaining egg whites carefully. Turn into the prepared pan. Bake 30 minutes or until browned and top springs back when pressed with the finger. Cool in the pan 10 minutes, run a spatula around the edge and turn out onto a cake rack. Turn right side up and finish cooling. Sprinkle with powdered sugar or cover with Apricot Glaze.

MARQUIS CHOCOLATE SPONGE CAKE

3½ squares (ounces) semi-
sweet chocolate
2 tablespoons cognac or
brewed coffee
4 tablespoons soft butter
3 egg yolks

½ cup plus 1 tablespoon
sugar
⅔ cup sifted cake flour
3 egg whites
⅛ teaspoon salt

Preheat oven to 350°. Place oven rack on middle level of oven. Grease an 8-inch layer cake pan and dust lightly with flour.

Break the chocolate into small pieces and combine in a small saucepan with the cognac or coffee. Place over hot water and stir with a wooden spoon until melted and smooth. Remove from the heat and beat in the butter, a little at a time, until smooth.

Beat the egg yolks, then add ½ cup sugar, beating with an electric mixer or wire whisk until thick and light. Fold in the flour carefully.

Beat the egg whites and salt until soft peaks form, then beat in the 1 tablespoon sugar until stiff but not dry. Fold the chocolate mixture into the flour mixture. Fold in half the egg whites, then fold in the remaining egg whites carefully. Turn into the pan. Bake 30 minutes or until a cake tester comes out clean. (The top will crack in baking.) Cool in the pan 5 minutes, then run a spatula around the edge and turn out. Turn right side up and finish cooling on a cake rack. Sprinkle with powdered sugar, or split, and fill with Butter Cream and cover with Chocolate Glaze.

HOT MILK SPONGE CAKE

1 cup sifted cake flour
¼ teaspoon salt
1 teaspoon baking powder
2 eggs

1 cup sugar
1 teaspoon vanilla extract
1 tablespoon butter
½ cup milk

Preheat oven to 350°. Grease only the bottom of an 8-inch square baking pan and dust lightly with flour.

Sift together the flour, salt and baking powder. Beat the eggs in a bowl until light and thick. Gradually beat in the sugar, then stir in the vanilla. Add the flour mixture gradually, stirring just until blended. Bring the butter and milk to a boil; add to the previous mixture, stirring steadily until smooth. Pour into the prepared pan. Bake 25 minutes or until a cake tester comes out clean. Cool on a cake rack.

BUTTER SPONGE CAKE

4 egg yolks
¾ cup sugar
2 teaspoons vanilla extract
1¼ cups sifted cake flour

4 egg whites
⅛ teaspoon salt
¼ cup melted butter, cooled

Preheat oven to 350°. Place oven rack in the middle level. Grease a 9-inch layer cake pan and dust lightly with flour.

Beat the egg yolks, then gradually add the sugar (reserving 2 tablespoons) beating with an electric mixer or wire whisk until thick and light. Beat in the vanilla. Carefully fold in the flour.

Beat the egg whites and salt until soft peaks form, then beat in the reserved sugar until stiff but not dry. Fold half the egg whites into the flour mixture, then fold in all the egg whites lightly. Fold in the melted butter. Turn into the pan. Bake 30 minutes or until browned and slightly shrunk away from the sides of the pan. Cool in the pan 5 minutes; run a spatula around the edge and turn out onto a cake rack. Turn right side up and let stand until cold. Sprinkle with powdered sugar, ice as you wish, or use for strawberry shortcake.

SPONGE CAKE
(WITH LEAVENING)

1⅓ cups sifted cake flour
½ teaspoon salt
½ teaspoon baking powder
1½ cups sifted very fine
   granulated sugar

6 egg yolks
¼ cup water
2 teaspoons lemon juice
6 egg whites
1 teaspoon cream of tartar

Preheat oven to 375°.

Sift together the flour, salt, baking powder and 1 cup sugar. Add the egg yolks, water and lemon juice. Beat just until smooth. Beat the egg whites and cream of tartar until soft peaks form, then beat in the remaining sugar gradually until very stiff. Fold in the egg yolk mixture carefully. Pour into an ungreased 10-inch spring form. Using a spoon or rubber spatula, cut through the batter to break up air pockets. Bake 35 minutes or until top springs back when pressed with the finger. Invert pan and let cool 2 hours. Run a spatula around the sides and center tube and turn out. Serve plain, or cut into layers and frost as you like.

CUSTARD-FILLED SPONGE ROLL

Sponge Roll

5 *egg yolks*
⅓ *cup sugar*
5 *egg whites*
⅓ *cup sifted flour*

⅛ *teaspoon salt*
½ *teaspoon baking powder*

Preheat the oven to 425°. Grease a jellyroll pan (11 by 17 inches), line with waxed paper, and grease the paper.

Beat the egg yolks, gradually adding the sugar; continue beating until light and fluffy. Beat the egg whites until stiff but not dry; heap on the egg yolks, but don't mix. Sift the flour, salt, and baking powder over the whites; fold in carefully but thoroughly. Turn into the prepared pan; spread evenly. Bake 12 minutes. Carefully turn out onto a towel; peel the paper from the cake. Roll up the cake in the towel until cool.

Custard Filling

6 *egg yolks*
¾ *cup sugar*
½ *cup sifted flour*
2 *teaspoons cornstarch*

3 *cups milk, scalded*
2 *teaspoons vanilla extract*
Powdered sugar

In a saucepan, beat together the egg yolks, sugar, flour, and cornstarch. Gradually add the hot milk, mixing steadily. Cook over low heat, mixing constantly, until thickened. Do not let boil. Remove from the heat and stir in the vanilla. Cool. Unroll the cake, spread filling on it, and roll up again. Sprinkle with powdered sugar. Cut into slices.

Serves 12–14.

CAKE ROLL

¾ cup sifted cake flour
¼ teaspoon salt
¾ teaspoon baking powder
4 eggs

¾ cup very fine granulated sugar
1 teaspoon vanilla extract
Confectioners' sugar

Preheat oven to 400°. Grease a jelly roll pan (15 by 10 by 1 inches). Line with waxed paper and grease again.

Sift together the flour, salt and baking powder. Beat the eggs until thick and light. Gradually beat in the sugar, until thick and fluffy. Stir in the vanilla, then fold in the flour mixture. Spread the batter evenly in the prepared pan. Bake 12 minutes, or until top springs back when pressed with the finger. Sprinkle a towel with confectioners' sugar and turn cake out onto it. Peel off the paper carefully and trim any crisp edges. Roll up the cake in the towel. Cool on a cake rack. Unroll and remove towel. Spread with desired filling and roll up again. Chill.

Filling

Jelly or Jam: Spread cake with 1 cup jelly and 1 cup whipped cream.

Strawberry: Spread cake with 1 cup sweetened whipped cream and 1 cup sliced strawberries.

Chocolate: Spread cake with Chocolate Cream Filling.

CHOCOLATE ROLL

(BISCUIT ROULÉ AU CHOCOLAT)

6 ounces sweet chocolate
3 tablespoons brewed coffee
5 egg yolks
¾ cup sugar
1 tablespoon cognac

5 egg whites
Cocoa
1½ cups heavy cream,
  whipped
1 teaspoon vanilla extract

Preheat the oven to 350°. Grease a jelly roll pan (11 by 17 inches), line it with waxed paper and grease the paper.

Melt the chocolate in the coffee over low heat; cool. Beat the egg yolks, gradually beat in the sugar until thick and light. Mix in the chocolate and cognac. Beat the egg whites until stiff but not dry; fold into the chocolate mixture but thoroughly. Turn into the prepared pan and spread evenly. Bake 15 minutes, or until a cake tester comes out clean. Do not over-bake. Cover the cake with a damp towel and place in the refrigerator for 1 hour.

Sprinkle a long piece of waxed paper with cocoa. Carefully turn out the cake and peel the paper from it. Mix the whipped cream with the vanilla and spread over the cake. Roll up the long way, by gently raising the edge of the waxed paper. Don't worry if the roll cracks—patch it with a little more cocoa or cover with whipped cream.

Serves 10–12.

COLOMBIAN COCOA ROLL

⅔ cup sifted cake flour
¼ teaspoon salt
¾ teaspoon baking powder
⅓ cup unsweetened cocoa

1 cup very fine granulated
  sugar
6 eggs
1 teaspoon vanilla extract
Confectioners' sugar

Preheat oven to 350°. Grease a jelly roll pan (17 by 10 by 1 inch). Line with waxed paper and grease again.

Sift together the flour, salt, baking powder, cocoa and ¼ cup sugar. Beat the eggs until thick and light. Beat in the remaining sugar gradually until very thick and smooth. Stir in the vanilla, then fold in the flour mixture a little at a time. Spread batter evenly in the prepared pan. Bake 18 minutes or until a cake tester comes out clean. Cool on a cake rack 3 minutes. Sprinkle a towel with confectioners' sugar and turn cake out on it. Carefully peel the paper from it and trim the edges if crisp. Roll up the cake in the towel. Continue cooling on a cake rack. Carefully unroll and remove the towel. Spread with Whipped Cream, Fluffy Chocolate Frosting, etc. and roll up again. Chill.

For a square thin layer cake, cool the cake on the towel, but don't roll up. Cut in 3 or 4 equal-sized pieces. Put together in layers with desired filling.

NUT ROLL

6 egg yolks
¾ cup sugar
1½ cups ground nuts
1 teaspoon baking powder
1 teaspoon vanilla extract

6 egg whites
Confectioners' sugar
2 cups heavy cream
2 tablespoons cognac

Preheat the oven to 350°. Grease a jelly roll pan (11 by 17 inches); line it with waxed paper and grease the paper.

Beat the egg yolks and sugar together until thick and light. Toss the nuts with the baking powder and stir into the yolk mixture with the vanilla. Beat the egg whites until stiff but not dry. Fold into the nut mixture. Spread evenly on the prepared pan. Bake 15 minutes, or until a cake tester comes out clean. Don't overbake.

Remove from the oven and cover with a damp towel until completely cool. Loosen from the pan. Sprinkle confectioners' sugar heavily on a piece of waxed paper. Turn out the cake and carefully peel the waxed paper from it. Whip the cream with 2 tablespoons confectioners' sugar. Stir in the cognac; spread on the cake and roll up lengthwise. The cake is very delicate, so don't worry if it cracks slightly in rolling. Cover outside with whipped cream, if desired.

Serves 8–10.

GENOISE

6 *eggs*
1 *cup sugar*
1 *cup sifted flour*

¼ *pound (1 stick) sweet*
  butter, melted and cooled
1 *teaspoon vanilla extract*

Preheat the oven to 350°. Grease two 9-inch layer cake pans and dust lightly with flour, or use a 9-inch tube pan.

Use an electric mixer if you have one, because this batter must be beaten a long time. Beat the eggs in a very large bowl, then beat in the sugar.

Place the bowl over, not in, a saucepan containing hot water. Beat until the egg mixture is almost tripled in volume. Scrape the bowl several times. Remove bowl from the saucepan and gently fold in the flour a little at a time. At the same time, fold in the butter and vanilla. Use a very light hand, or an electric mixer set at lowest speed, so as not to break the air cells. Turn into the pans or pan. Bake layers 25 minutes, tube pan 35 minutes, or until the top springs back when pressed with the finger. Invert onto a cake rack, remove pans and let cool.

Variations

Chocolate Gênoise: Use ½ cup sifted unsweetened cocoa and ½ cup sifted flour in place of all the flour. Sift together before adding. Proceed as directed.

Nut Gênoise: Add ½ cup ground nuts when adding the flour.

TUBE CAKE

3 *cups sifted cake flour*
1 *teaspoon salt*
2 *teaspoons baking powder*
1¾ *cups very fine granulated*
  sugar

1 *cup (2 sticks) butter or*
  margarine
½ *cup milk*
1 *teaspoon almond extract*
4 *egg yolks*
3 *egg whites*

Preheat oven to 375°. Grease a 9-inch tube pan and dust lightly with flour.

Sift together the flour, salt, baking powder and sugar. Cream the butter; sift the flour mixture over it, then pour milk and almond extract over all. Stir to dampen, then beat very well. Add the egg yolks and whites; beat again until very smooth. Turn into the prepared pan. Bake 50 minutes ar until a cake tester comes out clean. Cool on a rack 20 minutes. Run a spatula around the sides and center, then turn out. Turn right side up and finish cooling on the rack. Sprinkle with confectioners' sugar or frost as you like.

PINEAPPLE UPSIDE-DOWN CAKE

Pineapple Mixture

1 8½-ounce can sliced
  pineapple
¼ cup melted butter

⅔ cup firmly packed
  brown sugar
½ cup flaked coconut

Preheat oven to 350°.

Drain the pineapple, reserving 2 tablespoons juice. Quarter the pineapple slices. Mix together the butter and sugar. Spread on the bottom of a 9-inch square baking pan. Sprinkle the reserved juice over it, then arrange the pineapple over it. Sprinkle with the coconut.

Batter

2 cups sifted cake flour
¼ teaspoon salt
2 teaspoons baking powder
¼ cup shortening

1 cup sugar
1 egg
¾ cup milk
¾ teaspoon almond extract

Sift together the flour, salt, and baking powder. Cream the shortening; gradually beat in the sugar until light and fluffy. Add the egg; beat well. Add the flour mixture alternately with the milk, beating well after each addition. Mix in the almond extract. Turn into the prepared pan. Bake 45 minutes, or until a cake tested comes out clean. Cool on a cake rack for 5 minutes. Invert on a serving dish and leave pan on cake for 2 minutes before removing. Serve warm, with whipped cream, if desired.

Serves 8–10.

COCOA LAYER CAKE

2¼ cups sifted cake flour
1 teaspoon salt
1 teaspoon baking soda
½ cup unsweetened cocoa
1¾ cups sugar

1½ cups buttermilk or sour milk
½ cup shortening
2 eggs
1 teaspoon vanilla extract

Preheat oven to 350°. Grease two 9-inch layer cake pans and dust lightly with flour.

Sift together the flour, salt and baking soda. Mix the cocoa, ½ cup sugar, and ½ cup buttermilk until smooth. Cream the shortening; gradually beat in the remaining sugar until light and fluffy. Beat in 1 egg at a time. Add the flour mixture alternately with the remaining buttermilk, beating after each addition. Blend in the cocoa mixture and vanilla. Divide batter evenly between the prepared pans. Bake 30 minutes or until a cake tester comes out clean. Cool on a cake rack for 10 minutes before removing from pan. Cool thoroughly before frosting with Chocolate, Seven Minute or Mint Frosting.

YELLOW CAKE

2¾ cups sifted cake flour
1 teaspoon salt
1 tablespoon baking powder
1⅔ cup sugar

⅔ cup butter or margarine
1 cup milk
2 eggs
1 teaspoon vanilla extract

Preheat oven to 350°. Grease two 9-inch layer cake pans and dust lightly with flour.

Sift together the flour, salt, baking powder and sugar. Cream the butter; sift the dry ingredients into it, mixing lightly. Gradually add ¾ cup of the milk; beat 2 minutes with an electric mixer at low speed or with a wooden spoon for 4 minutes. Add the remaining milk, the eggs and vanilla. Beat 1 minute longer. Divide evenly between the pans. Bake 30 minutes or until a cake tester comes out clean. Cool on a cake rack for 10 minutes, then turn out onto the rack to cool completely. Frost as you like.

WHITE CAKE

2¾ cups sifted cake flour
¾ teaspoon salt
4 teaspoons baking powder
4 egg whites
1½ cups sifted fine granulated sugar

¾ cup shortening
1 cup milk
2 tablespoons heavy cream
1 teaspoon vanilla extract
½ teaspoon almond extract

Preheat oven to 350°. Great two 9-inch layer cake pans and dust lightly with flour.

Sift together the flour, salt and baking powder. Beat the egg whites until foamy. Gradually beat in ½ cup sugar until soft peaks are formed. Cream the shortening; gradually beat in the remaining sugar until light and fluffy. Add the flour mixture alternately with the milk and cream, beating after each addition. Stir in the vanilla and almond extracts, then mix in the beaten egg whites. Divide batter evenly between the prepared pans. Bake 30 minutes or until a cake tester comes out clean. Cool on a cake rack 10 minutes before removing from pans. Cool thoroughly before frosting as you like.

WHITE BUTTER CAKE

½ pound (2 sticks) butter
1⅔ cups sugar
2⅔ cups sifted flour
1 teaspoon vanilla extract

8 egg whites
⅛ teaspoon salt
¼ teaspoon cream of tartar

Preheat oven to 350°. Grease a 9-inch tube pan and dust lightly with flour.

Cream the butter; gradually beat in ⅔ cup sugar until light and fluffy. Beat in half the flour and all the vanilla.

Beat the egg whites, salt and cream of tartar until soft peaks are formed. Beat in the remaining sugar, 1 tablespoon at a time until very stiff. Fold half the egg whites into the butter mixture. Pile the remaining egg whites on top and sift the remaining flour over them. Fold together gently. Bake 50 minutes or until browned and cake shrinks away from the sides of the pan. Cool on a cake rack 30 minutes, then turn out to finish cooling on the rack.

EGG YOLK CAKE

2¼ cups sifted cake flour	1 cup sugar
¾ teaspoon salt	3 egg yolks
2½ teaspoons baking powder	1 cup milk
¼ pound (1 stick) butter or margarine	1 teaspoon vanilla extract

Preheat oven to 375°. Grease two 8-inch layer cake pans and dust lightly with flour.

Sift together the flour, salt and baking powder. Cream the butter; gradually beat in the sugar until light and fluffy. Beat in 1 egg yolk at a time. Add the flour mixture alternately with the milk; beat well after each addition. Mix in the vanilla. Divide batter evenly between the prepared pans. Bake 25 minutes or until a cake tester comes out clean. Cool on a cake rack for 10 minutes before removing from pan. Cool thoroughly before frosting, as you like.

LEMON SYRUP CAKE

1½ cups sifted cake flour	¾ cup buttermilk or sour milk
⅛ teaspoon salt	¼ cup seedless raisins
1 teaspoon baking soda	2 teaspoons grated lemon rind
4 tablespoons butter	1 tablespoon rum
1¼ cups packed brown sugar	3 tablespoons lemon juice
1 egg, beaten	

Preheat oven to 350°.

Sift together the flour, salt and baking soda.

Cream the butter; gradually beat in 1 cup of the brown sugar until very light and fluffy. Beat in the egg. Add the flour mixture alternately with the buttermilk, beating after each addition. Mix in the raisins and lemon rind. Pour into a greased 8-inch square cake pan. Bake 30 minutes or until cake pulls away from the sides of the pan and is browned.

While the cake is baking, prepare the syrup. Bring the rum, lemon juice and remaining brown sugar to a boil. Mix until sugar dissolves. Cool.

Place cake on a cake rack and immediately pour the syrup over it. Serve warm or cold, cut into squares.

RAISIN-FILLED CAKE

3 cups sifted flour	3/4 cup chopped nuts
2 teaspoons cream of tartar	3/4 cup (1½ sticks) butter
2 teaspoons baking soda	3/4 cup dark brown sugar
½ cup water	3 eggs, beaten
1 tablespoon cornstarch	3/4 cup milk
7/8 cup sugar	1½ teaspoons vanilla extract
1¼ cups seedless raisins	

Sift together the flour, cream of tartar and baking soda.

In a saucepan, mix the water, cornstarch, and ½ cup sugar. Cook over low heat, stirring constantly until thickened. Mix in the raisins and nuts. Cool while preparing the batter. Preheat oven to 375°.

Cream the butter, gradually adding the brown sugar and the remaining white sugar. Beat in the eggs until light and fluffy. Add the dry ingredients to the butter mixture alternately with the milk. Stir in the vanilla. Pour half the batter into a buttered 8-inch square pan. Spread the raisin mixture over it and cover with the remaining batter. Bake for 35 minutes, or until a cake tester comes out clean. Cool on a cake rack. Cut into 2-inch squares.

RAISIN TEA CAKE

1½ cups seedless raisins,
    white and dark
¼ cup cognac
½ pound (2 sticks) butter
1 cup sugar

6 egg yolks
1 teaspoon vanilla extract
6 egg whites
⅛ teaspoon salt
2 cups sifted flour

Preheat oven to 350°. Grease a 9-inch tube pan and dust lightly with flour.

Soak the raisins in the cognac 1 hour. Drain.

Cream the butter; gradually beat in ¼ cup sugar until light and fluffy. Beat in 1 egg yolk at a time. Mix in the vanilla and raisins.

Beat the egg whites and salt until soft peaks are formed, then beat in 1 tablespoon of the remaining sugar at a time. Continue beating until very stiff. Fold half the egg whites into the butter mixture. Pile the remaining egg whites over it, then sift the flour over them. Fold together carefully. Turn into the pan. Bake 50 minutes or until browned and cake shrunk away from the sides of the pan. Cool on a cake rack 20 minutes then turn out and finish cooling on the rack.

ALMOND TEA CAKE

¾ cup whole blanched
    almonds
4 whole eggs
4 egg yolks
1 cup sugar
1 teaspoon vanilla extract

2 tablespoons sifted
    cornstarch
1½ cups sifted flour
⅛ teaspoon nutmeg
½ pound (2 sticks) butter,
    melted and cooled

Preheat oven to 350°. Grease a 9-inch tube pan and dust lightly with flour. Arrange the almonds on the bottom of the pan.

In a large bowl, combine the eggs, egg yolks and sugar. Set the bowl over, not in, hot water and beat with an electric or rotary beater until almost tripled in bulk. Remove from heat. Stir in the vanilla gently. Sift the cornstarch, flour, and nutmeg over the top and fold in gently, adding the butter gradually at the same time. Turn into the pan. Bake 50 minutes or until browned and cake shrinks away from the sides of the pan. Cool on a cake rack 20 minutes, then turn out to finish cooling.

Variation

Spanish Tea Cake: Grate 3 ounces semi-sweet chocolate and mix it with 1 teaspoon cinnamon. Pour one third the batter in the pan, sprinkle with one half the chocolate mixture, cover with half the remaining batter, sprinkle with remaining chocolate mixture and cover with remaining batter. Proceed as directed.

DUNDEE CAKE

1¼ cups sifted flour
¼ teaspoon salt
½ teaspoon baking powder
½ cup currants
½ cup seedless raisins
¼ pound (1 stick) butter or margarine
⅓ cup sugar
2 eggs

¼ cup chopped blanched almonds
2 tablespoons orange juice
¼ cup chopped candied orange peel
¼ cup whole candied cherries
¼ cup whole blanched almonds

Preheat oven to 300°. Grease a 9-inch loaf pan; line it with heavy paper or aluminum foil and grease again.

Sift together the flour, salt and baking powder. Mix in the currants and raisins. Cream the butter; gradually add the sugar, beating until light and fluffy. Add 1 egg at a time, beating well after each addition. Mix in the chopped almonds; add the orange juice alternately with the flour mixture. Stir until well-blended. Mix in the orange peel. Turn into the prepared pan. Arrange the cherries and almonds on top. Bake 1¼ hours or until a cake tester comes out clean. Cover the top with a

piece of aluminum foil when top begins to brown. Cool on a
cake rack 15 minutes before removing from pan. Finish cooling
on the cake rack.

ENGLISH SEED CAKE

2 cups sifted cake flour	4 eggs
¼ teaspoon cream of tartar	1 egg yolk
¼ teaspoon salt	¼ teaspoon mace
½ pound sweet butter	½ teaspoon vanilla extract
1 cup sugar	3 tablespoons caraway seeds

Preheat the oven to 350°. Line a greased 9-by-5-inch loaf
pan with aluminum foil, and let the foil extend an inch or so
along the top edge.

Sift together the flour, cream of tartar and salt. Cream the
butter. Gradually beat in the sugar until very fluffy and light.
Add 1 egg at a time, beating after each addition. Beat in the
egg yolk, mace and vanilla. Fold in the flour mixture gradually
until thoroughly blended, then fold in the caraway seeds. Turn
into the lined pan. Bake 1¼ hours or until golden brown and
a cake tester comes out clean. Cool in the pan on a cake rack
for 10 minutes. Lift the cake out by the foil and finish cooling
on the rack. Carefully peel the foil from the cake.

ORANGE CAKE

3 cups sifted cake flour	rind
½ teaspoon salt	1⅔ cups sugar
1 tablespoon baking powder	2 eggs
¾ teaspoon baking soda	¼ cup milk
⅔ cup butter or margarine	1 cup orange juice
1 tablespoon grated orange	

Preheat oven to 375° Grease two 9-inch layer cake pans
and dust lightly with flour.

Sift together the flour, salt, baking powder and baking soda.
Cream the butter, then mix in the orange rind. Gradually beat

in the sugar until light and fluffy. Add 1 egg at a time, beating well after each addition. Add the flour mixture alternately with the milk and orange juice, beating until smooth after each addition. Divide batter evenly between the prepared pans. Bake 25 minutes or until a cake tester comes out clean. Cool on a cake rack 10 minutes before removing from pan. Cool thoroughly before frosting with Orange Butter Frosting.

POUND CAKE

2 cups flour	6 egg yolks
⅛ teaspoon salt	1 teaspoon vanilla extract
½ pound soft butter	or ½ teaspoon mace
1 cup sugar	6 egg whites

Preheat oven to 350°. Grease a 9-inch tube pan and dust lightly with flour.

Sift together the flour and salt. Cream the butter; beat in ½ cup sugar until very light and fluffy. Add 1 egg yolk at a time, beating well after each addition. Beat in the vanilla or mace.

Beat the egg whites until soft peaks form, then beat in 1 tablespoon of the remaining sugar at a time until very stiff. Pile the egg whites on top of the butter mixture, then sift the flour over the egg whites. Fold together carefully but thoroughly. Turn into the prepared pan. Bake 45 minutes or until browned and slightly shrunk away from the sides of pan. Cool on a cake rack 20 minutes, then run a spatula around the edges and turn out onto the rack. Pound cake should not be cut for several hours after it is baked.

VIRGINIA POUND CAKE

2¼ cups sifted cake flour	½ teaspoon mace
½ teaspoon salt	1 teaspoon vanilla extract
1 teaspoon baking powder	4 eggs
1 cup (2 sticks) butter	¼ cup milk
1¼ cups very fine	
granulated sugar	

Preheat oven to 325°. Grease a 9-inch loaf pan and dust lightly with flour.

Sift together the flour, salt and baking powder. Cream the butter until very fluffy. Very gradually beat in the sugar until extremely light. Mix in the mace and vanilla. Add 1 egg at a time, beating well after each addition. Add the flour mixture alternately with the milk, beating after each addition. Turn into the prepared pan. Bake 1¼ hours or until a cake tester comes out clean. Cool on a cake rack 20 minutes before removing from pan. Turn right side up to finish cooling. Bake the cake the day before it is to be served, if possible.

LIGHT FRUIT CAKE

½ pound (2 sticks) butter
1 cup sugar
6 egg yolks
1 teaspoon vanilla extract
¼ teaspoon mace
2 cups flour
⅛ teaspoon salt

1½ cups mixed chopped candied fruit
½ cup coarsely chopped walnuts or pecans
½ teaspoon cream of tartar
6 egg whites

Preheat oven to 350°. Grease a 9-inch tube pan and dust lightly with flour.

Cream the butter and ¼ cup sugar until light and fluffy. Beat in 1 egg yolk at a time, then the vanilla and mace. Stir in 1¾ cups flour and the salt. Toss the fruit and nuts with the cream of tartar and remaining flour.

Beat the egg whites until soft peaks are formed, then beat in 1 tablespoon of the remaining sugar at a time until very soft. Fold half the egg whites into the butter mixture, then pile remaining egg whites over it. Sprinkle the fruit mixture on top, then fold all together gently. Turn into the pan. Bake 1 hour and 5 minutes or until browned and cake shrunk away from sides of pan. Cool on a cake rack before removing from pan.

UNBAKED (FROZEN) FRUITCAKE

¼ cup flour
¼ teaspoon salt
½ cup sugar
½ cup cold milk
1½ cups milk, scalded
2 eggs
¼ cup cognac

1 cup chopped pecans or
    walnuts
2 cups macaroon crumbs
1 cup chopped candied fruit
½ cup chopped candied
    cherries
1 cup heavy cream

Sift the flour, salt and sugar into a saucepan. Blend in the cold milk until smooth, then gradually stir in the scalded milk. Cook over low heat, stirring constantly, until mixture boils, then cook 5 minutes longer, stirring frequently.

Beat the eggs lightly in a bowl; gradually add the hot mixture, stirring steadily to prevent curdling. Return to saucepan; cook, stirring steadily, for 2 minutes, but do not let boil. Cool. Mix in the cognac, nuts, crumbs, fruit and cherries. Whip the cream lightly and fold into the fruit mixture. Turn into a buttered 9-by 5-inch loaf pan. Wrap carefully in aluminum foil. Freeze at least 24 hours before serving but cake will keep frozen one month. Let stand at room temperature 30 minutes before serving.

To serve, run a spatula around the edges. Turn out onto a serving dish. Decorate with nuts, cherries and whipped cream, if desired.

Serves 10–12.

CUPCAKES

2 cups sifted flour
½ teaspoon salt
2 teaspoons baking powder
½ cup shortening

1¼ cups sugar
2 eggs
1 cup milk
1 teaspoon vanilla extract

Preheat oven to 375° Line 24 muffin tins with paper cupcake liners, or grease and dust lightly with flour.

Sift together the flour, salt and baking powder. Cream the shortening; gradually beat in the sugar until light and fluffy. Beat in 1 egg at a time. Add the flour mixture and milk alternately, beating well after each addition. Stir in the vanilla. Spoon into the prepared pans. Bake 20 minutes or until a cake tester comes out clean. Cool on a cake rack. Frost as you like.

DEVIL'S FOOD CUPCAKES

1 cup sifted cake flour
½ teaspoon salt
½ teaspoon baking soda
¼ cup unsweetened cocoa
4 tablespoons (½ stick) butter

½ cup buttermilk or sour milk
½ teaspoon vanilla extract
2 egg yolks
1 egg white

Preheat oven to 350°. Line 18 muffin pans with paper cupcake liners, or grease and dust lightly with flour.

Sift together the flour, salt, baking soda and cocoa. Cream the butter; mix in the flour mixture. Add half the buttermilk and the vanilla; beat well. Add the remaining buttermilk, the egg yolks and white; beat well again. Spoon into the prepared pans. Bake 25 minutes or until a cake tester comes out clean. Cool on a cake rack. Frost, if you like with Chocolate or White Frosting.

BABA AU RHUM

1 cake or envelope yeast
1 tablespoon sugar
¼ cup lukewarm water
2 cups sifted flour
½ teaspoon salt
4 eggs, beaten

¼ cup light cream, scalded and cooled to lukewarm
⅔ cup soft butter
2 tablespoons currants or seedless raisins

Combine the yeast, sugar and water in a cup. Let stand 5 minutes. Sift the flour and salt into a bowl and make a well in the center. Pour in the eggs, yeast mixture and cream. Mix in the flour with the hand until a dough is formed. Pick up the dough and slap it down until smooth and elastic. Place in a bowl, cover with a towel and let rise in a warm place until double in bulk, about 1 hour. Punch the dough down and work in the butter and currants. Beat with the hand for 5 minutes. Transfer the dough to a fluted, buttered 7-inch ring mold. Cover and let rise in a warm place until double in bulk, about 1 hour. Preheat the oven to 450°.

Bake 10 minutes at 450°, then reduce the heat to 350° and bake 35 minutes longer or until browned and a cake tester comes out clean. Unmold onto a serving dish immediately and pour the Rum Syrup over it, which should be prepared while the Baba is baking.

Syrup

1½ cups water   ½ cup rum
1 cup sugar

Cook the water and sugar over high heat until thick and syrupy, about 5–7 minutes. Remove from the heat and stir in the rum. Pour over the Baba and let stand 3–4 hours. To serve aflame, sprinkle with 3 tablespoons confectioners' sugar and pour ¼ cup warm rum over it and set aflame.

NOTE: Small Babas can be made by spooning the dough into individual molds or muffin tins. Bake in a 375° oven for 20 minutes. Makes about 10. Babas can be served with ice cream, stewed fruits or whipped cream.

SAVARIN

1 envelope or package yeast   ½ teaspoon salt
¼ cup lukewarm water   2 cups sifted flour
¼ cup milk, scalded and   4 eggs
    cooled   ⅔ cup butter, softened
3 tablespoons sugar

Soften the yeast in the water, then stir in the milk, sugar, salt and ¾ cup of the flour. Work in the eggs and enough of the remaining flour to make a soft batter. Beat vigorously for a few minutes. Cover and let rise in a warm place for 45 minutes. Beat in the butter until smooth. Spread in a buttered 9-inch savarin or ring mold. Cover and let rise until double in bulk. Bake in a preheated 375° oven 45 minutes or until browned and shrunk away from the sides of the pan. Carefully turn out onto a serving dish and pour the syrup over it.

Syrup

1½ cups strong tea
2 cups sugar
3 slices orange

3 slices lemon
¼ cup cognac or rum

Cook the tea, sugar, orange and lemon until syrupy. Discard fruit and add liquor. Spoon over the savarin until most of the syrup is absorbed. Fill the center with sweetened whipped cream.

REFRIGERATOR COFFEE CAKE DOUGH

2 packages yeast
¼ cup lukewarm water
¼ cup milk, scalded and
    cooled
¼ cup sugar
½ teaspoon salt

½ cup sour cream
1 teaspoon vanilla extract
2 egg yolks, beaten
3 cups flour (about)
¾ cup (1½ sticks) butter,
    softened

Stir the yeast into the water; let stand 5 minutes. Mix in the milk, sugar, salt, sour cream, vanilla and egg yolks. Add just enough flour to make a soft dough—it may not be necessary to use all the flour. Work in the butter. Knead on a lightly floured surface until very smooth and elastic. If too sticky, use a little more flour. Form into a ball, place in a bowl, cover and chill 4 hours or overnight. If chilled overnight, punch down twice. Use as directed in the following recipes.

Schnecken

¾ cup packed brown sugar
½ cup chopped pecans or
    walnuts

½ cup seedless raisins
1 teaspoon cinnamon

Mix all the ingredients together. Divide dough into two pieces. Roll out each half into a rectangle ¼ inch thick. Sprinkle half the sugar mixture on each piece and roll up tightly like a jelly roll. Seal the edges with a little water or beaten egg. Cut in ½-inch slices. Arrange on a buttered baking sheet, leaving about 1 inch space between each. Cover with a towel and let rise until double in bulk, about 30 minutes.

Bake in a preheated 375° oven 20 minutes or until browned.

Makes about 3 dozen.

Coffee Cake Wreath

Divide dough into three pieces. Roll each piece into a long strip, then braid the strips. Shape into a circle. Place on a buttered baking pan. Cover with a towel and let rise 30 minutes. Brush with melted butter. Bake in a preheated 375° oven 30 minutes or until browned.

COFFEE CRUMB CAKE

2 cups sifted flour	1 egg, beaten
1 teaspoon salt	1 cup milk
½ cup sugar	⅓ cup vegetable oil
2 teaspoons baking powder	

Preheat oven to 375°.

Mix and sift flour, salt, sugar, and baking powder into a bowl. Make a well in the center and into it put the egg, milk and oil. Stir only enough to dampen flour (batter should appear lumpy). Pour into a 10-inch pie plate. Sprinkle with the crumb topping. Bake 35 minutes or until brown.

Topping

Mix ¼ cup flour, ½ cup sugar and 1 teaspoon cinnamon in a bowl. Cut in 2 tablespoons butter with a pastry blender or 2 knives until the consistency of corn meal.

Tortes

AUSTRIAN CHOCOLATE TORTE

15 squares (ounces) semi-
 sweet chocolate
⅔ cup butter
4 egg yolks

1 teaspoon cinnamon
1 tablespoon sifted
 cornstarch
4 egg whites
3 tablespoons sugar

Preheat oven to 425°. Combine the chocolate and butter in the top of a double boiler; place over hot water until melted, stirring until smooth. Cool 10 minutes.

Beat the egg yolks until thick, then mix in the melted chocolate, cinnamon, sugar, and cornstarch. Beat the egg whites until stiff but not dry; fold into the chocolate mixture. Turn into an ungreased, 8-inch spring-form pan. Bake 20 minutes. Cool on a cake rack and remove sides of pan.

Frosting

4 squares (ounces) semi-
 sweet chocolate
3 tablespoons light corn
 syrup

1½ teaspoons cognac
¼ cup sliced Brazil nuts
 or almonds

Combine the chocolate, syrup, and cognac in the top of a double boiler; place over hot water and stir until melted. Cool 10 minutes; then ice the torte. Sprinkle the nuts on top.
 Serves 10–12.

VIENNESE COCOA TORTE

⅓ cup sifted unsweetened
 cocoa
1 cup ground almonds
6 eggs
⅔ cup sugar

1 teaspoon vanilla extract
⅓ cup melted butter,
 cooled
¼ cup cognac

49

Preheat oven to 350°. Grease only the bottom of a 9-inch tube pan.

Mix together the cocoa and nuts.

In a large bowl, beat the eggs and sugar. Set over, not in, a saucepan of hot water and beat with an electric or rotary beater until tripled in volume. Stir in the vanilla. Remove from the heat. Fold in the nut mixture and melted butter carefully. Turn into the pan. Bake 45 minutes, or until top springs back when pressed with the finger. Cool on a cake rack for several hours. Run a spatula around the edges and turn out. Sprinkle with the cognac. Cover with whipped cream or Chocolate Whipped Cream.

APRICOT MERINGUE TORTE

6 egg whites	1½ cups sifted flour
1½ cups sugar	1 pound apricot jam
⅔ cup melted cooled butter	

Start preparing the torte the day before you want to serve it.

Preheat oven to 425°. Grease on 8-inch spring-form and line it with waxed paper.

Beat the egg whites until peaks form; gradually add the sugar, beating until stiff but not dry. Fold in the butter and flour alternately, ending with the flour. Turn into the prepared pan. Bake 45 minutes; cool in the pan on a cake rack overnight.

Remove cake from pan and peel off the paper. Split cake into three or four layers and spread jam between them. Preheat oven to 350°.

Meringue

2 egg whites	½ cup sugar

Beat the egg whites until peaks form; add the sugar, gradually beating in until stiff but not dry. Spread over top and

sides of cake. Place in oven and turn off the heat at once. Let stand in oven with door closed for 3 hours. Cool.
Serves 8–10.

VENEZUELAN BANANA TORTE

5 bananas
⅛ teaspoon salt
½ cup sugar
2 tablespoons butter

2 tablespoons lime or lemon juice
½ teaspoon nutmeg
1 cup whipped cream
1 8-inch baked pastry shell

Mash the bananas very smooth, or purée in an electric blender. Combine with the salt, sugar, and butter in a saucepan; bring to a boil. Cool, and fold in the lime or lemon juice, nutmeg, and whipped cream. Turn into the pie shell. Chill.
Serves 6–8.

VIENNESE POPPY SEED TORTE

1½ cups poppy seeds
6 egg whites
1 cup sugar
6 egg yolks
⅔ cup vegetable oil

1½ cups dry bread crumbs
2 teaspoons baking powder
¼ teaspoon salt
1 teaspoon vanilla

Place poppy seeds in a saucepan with enough water to cover; bring to a boil over medium heat and boil 30 minutes, adding more water if necessary. Drain thoroughly and cool. Beat egg whites until soft peaks form; gradually add ¼ cup of the sugar; continue beating until stiff but not dry.

Beat the egg yolks until thick and lemon-colored; gradually beat in the remaining sugar, then the oil. Mix in the poppy seeds. Mix together the bread crumbs, baking powder, and salt. Blend into poppy seed–egg yolk mixture. Fold into the meringue mixture and add the vanilla. Turn into an ungreased 10-inch tube pan; bake in a preheated 325° oven for 1 hour. Invert over bottle or funnel to cool.

ITALIAN CHESTNUT TORTE

(TORTA DE CASTAGNE)

1½ pounds chestnuts
6 tablespoons butter
½ cup sugar
3 egg yolks
¾ cup sifted cake flour

2 teaspoons baking powder
¼ cup sliced almonds
2 tablespoons cognac
3 egg whites, stiffly beaten

Cut a crisscross in the pointed end of the chestnuts. Cover with water, bring to a boil and cook over low heat 40 minutes. Drain, cool slightly, peel and remove inner skin. Purée in an electric blender or force through a sieve. (You should have about 1 cup purée.) Preheat oven to 375°.

Cream the butter and sugar together until fluffy. Add 1 yolk at a time, beating after each addition. Beat in the chestnuts until smooth, then the flour, baking powder, almonds and cognac. Fold in the egg whites. Turn into two greased 8-inch layer cake pans. Bake 35 minutes, or until a cake tester comes out clean and cake shrinks away from sides of pan. Cool in the pans on a cake rack for 15 minutes, then turn out onto rack until completely cold. Fill and frost with the following recipe.

Frosting

2 teaspoons instant coffee
1 tablespoon hot water
4 tablespoons butter

2 cups sifted confectioners'
    sugar
1 tablespoon cognac
2 tablespoons heavy cream

Dissolve the coffee in the water. Cream the butter, gradually adding the sugar. Beat in the coffee, cognac and cream.

ITALIAN CHESTNUT REFRIGERATOR TORTE

(GATO DE CASTAGNE)

1 pound chestnuts
2 eggs
½ cup sugar
2 cups milk

1 square (ounce)
unsweetened chocolate
3 tablespoons cognac
1 teaspoon vanilla extract
1 cup heavy cream

Cut a crisscross in the pointed end of the chestnuts. Cover with water, bring to a boil and cook over low heat 40 minutes. Drain, cool slightly, peel and remove inner skin. Purée in an electric blender or force through a sieve.

Beat the eggs and sugar in the top of a double boiler. Stir in the milk and the chocolate, broken into small pieces. Place over hot water and cook, stirring constantly until thickened. Remove from the heat. Beat in the chestnuts, 1 tablespoon cognac and the vanilla. Cool slightly, then turn into a well-greased 7-inch tube pan. Chill 4 hours or until firm. Carefully unmold onto a serving dish. Fill center with the cream, whipped and flavored with remaining cognac.

Serves 6–8.

SWISS TORTE

3 egg whites
⅛ teaspoon salt
⅛ teaspoon cream of tartar
1 teaspoon vanilla extract

¾ cup fine granulated sugar
½ cup blanched ground nuts
¼ cup sifted cornstarch

Grease and dust with flour the bottom of two 9-inch cake pans with removable bottoms or grease and dust with flour a baking pan. As a guide, press a 9-inch layer cake onto it.

Beat the egg whites, salt, cream of tartar and vanilla until soft peaks form. Beat in 1 tablespoon of sugar at a time until ½ cup is used up and meringue is very stiff. Mix together the nuts, cornstarch and remaining sugar. Fold into the meringue.

Divide between the two pans or spread on the baking pan circles.

Bake in a preheated 325° oven 35 minutes or until dry to the touch. Cool. Put layers together with the following recipe.

Filling

6 *ounces semi-sweet* *chocolate*	¼ *pound butter, softened* 1 *egg yolk*
2 *tablespoons strong coffee*	1 *tablespoon cognac*

Melt the chocolate in the coffee, stirring until smooth. Cool. Cream the butter until fluffy, then beat in the chocolate, egg yolk and cognac. Spread between the layers. Chill. This torte is especially good if made the day before it is to be served.

AUSTRIAN FILBERT TORTE

½ *pound (1¾ cups) filberts* *(hazel nuts)*	¾ *cup sugar* 10 *egg yolks*
6 *egg whites*	¼ *cup cognac*
⅛ *teaspoon salt*	

Preheat oven to 350°. Grease the bottoms only of two 9-inch layer cake pans, line with waxed paper and grease paper. Grind the nuts very fine (in an electric blender or Mouli grater).

Beat the egg whites and salt until soft peaks form, then beat in 1 tablespoon sugar at a time until very stiff. Beat the egg yolks and 1 tablespoon cognac lightly. Fold about ¼ of the egg whites into the egg yolks. Pile the remaining egg whites over it and sprinkle the filberts on top. Fold together carefully but thoroughly. Divide between the lined pans.

Bake 30 minutes, or until delicately browned and top springs back when pressed with the finger. Cool on a cake rack 30 minutes. Carefully run a spatula around the edges and turn cakes out onto the rack. Peel the paper from the bottoms. Sprinkle with the remaining cognac. The torte may be put together and covered with Mocha Butter Cream or Coffee-Flavored Whipped Cream.

AUSTRIAN LINZER (ALMOND) TORTE

1¼ cups sifted flour
½ teaspoon cinnamon
½ cup sugar
2 tablespoons unsweetened
   cocoa
⅓ pound (1 cup) shelled
   almonds
½ pound butter

2 egg yolks
2 hard-cooked egg yolks,
   sieved
1 teaspoon grated lemon rind
1 teaspoon vanilla extract
1½ cups raspberry jam
3 tablespoons heavy cream

Sift together the flour, cinnamon, sugar and cocoa. Grind the almonds very fine (use an electric blender or a Mouli Grater). Mix into the sifted ingredients. Make a well in the center and into it put the butter, raw yolks, mashed cooked yolks, lemon rind and vanilla. Mix with the hand until a dough is formed. Chill 15 minutes.

Roll out two-thirds of the dough (between two sheets of waxed paper) to fit an 8-inch straight-sided cake pan. Spread with the jam. Roll out the remaining dough and cut into ¼-inch wide strips. Place over the jam in a lattice pattern. Brush the strips and edge with the cream. Chill 1 hour. Bake in a preheated 350° oven 45 minutes or until lightly browned. Cool.

SWISS ALMOND TORTE

1¼ cups (2½ sticks) butter
1¼ cups sugar
1 egg
1¾ cups sifted flour

2¼ cups ground almonds
1 teaspoon almond extract
2 tablespoons heavy cream

Preheat oven to 325°.

Cream the butter and sugar together. Mix in the egg, then the flour, 2 cups almonds, and the almond extract until smooth. Turn into a buttered 9-inch spring form. Brush the top with the cream and sprinkle with the remaining almonds.

Bake 50 minutes, or until delicately browned and a cake tester comes out clean. Cool before removing from pan.

Serves 8–10.

CARROT TORTE

¼ cup dry bread crumbs

12 egg yolks

¾ cup sugar

¼ cup grated carrots

¾ cup ground almonds

½ cup grated apple

1 tablespoon cognac

12 egg whites

Preheat the oven to 375° Grease a 10-inch spring form and dust with the bread crumbs.

Beat the egg yolks; add the sugar, beating until light and fluffy. Stir in the carrots, almonds, apple and cognac.

Beat the egg whites until stiff but not dry; fold into the carrot mixture. Turn into the pan. Bake 45 minutes, or until a cake tester comes out clean. Cool before removing from pan. Cover with whipped cream.

Serves 10–12.

ITALIAN RUM TORTE

ZUPPA INGLESE

2 tablespoons cornstarch

¼ teaspoon salt

½ cup sugar

2 cups milk

3 egg yolks

1 teaspoon vanilla extract

36 lady fingers

1 cup rum

1 cup heavy cream

1 tablespoon confectioners' sugar

Sift the cornstarch, salt and sugar into a saucepan. Gradually beat in the milk, then the egg yolks. Cook over low heat, mixing steadily, until thickened and smooth, but don't boil the mixture. Remove from the heat and beat in the vanilla. Strain if there are any lumps. Cool.

Line the bottom of an 11-inch deep pie plate closely with

some lady fingers; pour ¼ cup rum over it. Cover with half the cooled custard. Make another layer of lady fingers (reserving some for the top), sprinkle with ¼ cup rum, spread remaining custard over it and cover with remaining lady fingers. Sprinkle with ¼ cup rum. Cover and chill 3–4 hours. Just before serving, pour the remaining rum over the top, and cover with the cream whipped with the confectioners' sugar.

Cookies

CREAM CHEESE COOKIES

1¾ cups sifted flour
½ teaspoon salt
½ teaspoon baking powder
1 3-ounce package cream cheese (at room temperature)
2 tablespoons sour cream

¼ pound (1 stick) butter
1 cup sugar
1 egg
1 teaspoon vanilla extract
3 tablespoons powdered sugar
2 teaspoons cinnamon

Sift together the flour, salt and baking powder. Beat the cream cheese and sour cream together until smooth and soft. Cream the butter; gradually beat in the sugar until light and fluffy. Mix in the egg and vanilla, then the cream cheese. Blend in the flour mixture. Shape into a ball, wrap in foil or waxed paper and chill overnight. Roll out the dough as thin as possible on a lightly floured surface. Cut into desired shapes with a floured cooky cutter. Arrange on greased baking sheets. Sprinkle with a mixture of the powdered sugar and cinnamon. Bake in a preheated 350° oven 12 minutes or until delicately browned. It is not necessary to bake all the dough at once. Keep in the refrigerator and bake as needed.

Makes about 5 dozen 3-inch cookies.

ENGLISH MOLASSES DROP COOKIES

1½ cups sifted cake flour
¼ teaspoon salt
¾ teaspoons baking soda
½ teaspoon cinnamon
¾ teaspoon ground ginger
¼ teaspoon nutmeg

¼ cup butter
½ cup sugar
1 egg yolk
¼ cup molasses
½ cup buttermilk

Sift together the flour, salt, baking soda, cinnamon, ginger and nutmeg. Cream the butter; gradually beat in the sugar until light and fluffy. Beat in the egg yolk then the molasses. Add the flour mixture alternately with the buttermilk, mixing well after each addition. Chill 1½ hours, or until stiff enough to hold its shape. Drop by the teaspoon onto greased baking sheets, leaving 2 inches between each. Bake in a preheated 400° oven 10 minutes or until delicately browned. Remove from pans with a spatula.

Makes about 3 dozen cookies.

Variations

Molasses Raisin Cookies: Add ½ cup seedless raisins to the batter before chilling. Proceed as directed.

Molasses Nut Cookies: Add ½ cup coarsely chopped nuts to the batter before chilling. Proceed as directed.

CRISP SUGAR COOKIES

3½ cups sifted cake flour
½ teaspoon salt
2½ teaspoons baking powder
¾ cup (1½ sticks) butter

1½ cups sugar
2 eggs
1½ teaspoons vanilla extract
1 tablespoon milk

Sift together the flour, salt and baking powder. Cream the butter; gradually beat in the sugar until light and fluffy. Beat in 1 egg at a time. Add the flour mixture alternately with the vanilla mixed with the milk. Form into a ball, wrap in foil or waxed paper and chill 4 hours or overnight.

Roll out ⅛ inch thick on a lightly floured surface. Cut with a floured cooky cutter and sprinkle with sugar—cinnamon too, if you like. Arrange on ungreased cooky sheets. Bake in a preheated 400° oven 8 minutes or until delicately browned.

Makes about 6 dozen 3-inch cookies.

VIENNA SUGAR COOKIES

(SABLÉ VIENNOIS)

1½ cups flour
2 teaspoons baking powder
¼ pound (1 stick) butter

1 cup sugar
3 egg yolks
1 teaspoon vanilla extract

Sift the flour and baking powder into a bowl. Make a well in the center and place the butter, sugar, egg yolks and vanilla in it. Using the hand, mix the ingredients in the well until smooth, then work in the flour. Chill for 2 hours.

Roll out on a lightly floured surface ¼ inch thick. Cut with a floured cooky cutter and transfer to a baking sheet with a spatula. Bake in a preheated 375° oven 8 minutes or until lightly browned. Cool on a cake rack for 5 minutes before removing from pan.

Makes about 36 3-inch cookies.

ALMOND COOKIES

1 cup sifted flour
⅛ teaspoon salt
⅓ cup sugar
½ cup ground blanched
  almonds
⅓ cup softened butter

1 egg
2 teaspoons grated lemon
  rind
3 tablespoons heavy cream
18 almonds, split

Sift the flour and salt into a bowl. Make a well in the center and into it put the sugar, almonds, butter, egg and lemon rind. Mix the ingredients in the well with a wooden spoon until smooth. With the hand, work in the flour. Form into a ball, wrap in foil or waxed paper and chill 2 hours. Roll out the dough ¼ inch thick on a lightly floured surface. Cut with a floured cooky cutter. Arrange on a greased baking sheet. Brush with the cream and gently press a half almond in the center of each cooky. Bake in a preheated 350° oven 10 minutes or until delicately browned.

Makes about 24 3-inch cookies.

CRISP BUTTER COOKIES

1 pound (4 sticks) butter	2 tablespoons cognac
¾ cup confectioners sugar	4½ cups sifted flour (about)
1 egg yolk	½ cup very fine sugar

Cream the butter; gradually add the sugar, beating until light and fluffy. Beat in the egg yolk and cognac. Work in enough of the flour to make a fairly firm dough. Form into two balls, wrap in foil or waxed paper and chill 3 hours.

Remove one ball at a time and roll ⅓ inch thick between two sheets of waxed paper. Cut into any shape you like with a floured cooky cutter. Work quickly, as dough becomes soft at room temperature. Arrange on ungreased cooky sheets. Bake in a preheated 350° oven 15 minutes or until edges begin to brown. Cool on a cake rack 10 minutes, then sprinkle with the fine sugar.

Makes about 4 dozen 3-inch cookies.

OATMEAL COOKIES

¾ cup sifted flour	½ cup packed brown sugar
½ teaspoon salt	1 egg, beaten
½ teaspoon baking soda	1½ cups quick-cooking
¼ pound (1 stick) butter	rolled oats, uncooked
½ cup granulated sugar	1 teaspoon vanilla extract

Sift together the flour, salt and baking soda. Cream the butter; gradually beat in the granulated and brown sugars until light and fluffy. Beat in the egg. Mix in the flour mixture, then the oats and vanilla. Shape into rolls 2 inches thick. Wrap in foil or waxed paper; chill until firm.

With a sharp knife, cut the rolls in ⅛-inch slices. Arrange on greased baking sheets leaving 1 inch between each. Bake in a preheated 400° oven 10 minutes. Cool on a cake rack.

Makes about 3 dozen cookies.

JAM COOKIES

½ pound (2 sticks) butter,
  at room temperature
½ teaspoon salt
1¾ cups thinly slivered
  blanched almonds

2½ cups sifted flour
½ cup heavy cream
Sugar
1½ cups raspberry jam

Cream the butter, then blend in the salt and almonds. Add the flour alternately with the cream. Form into two balls, wrap in foil or waxed paper and chill 1 hour.

Heavily sprinkle a pastry cloth, piece of waxed paper or a board with sugar and roll out each pice of dough very thin. Cut into circles with a one or two-inch round, floured cooky cutter. Using a smaller cutter or shot glass, cut out the centers of half the circles. Transfer cookies to greased cooky sheets with a spatula. Bake in a preheated 350° (with oven rack on middle level) 8 minutes or until delicately browned. Transfer cookies to a cake rack with a spatula and cool. Spread solid cookes wth jam and cover with the cut-out cooky. Fill centers with a little more jam.

Makes about 20 2-inch cookies.

SWEDISH HONEY COOKIES

2 cups sifted flour
½ teaspoon salt
½ teaspoon baking soda
¾ teaspoon ginger
½ teaspoon cinnamon

½ teaspoon nutmeg
¼ pound (1 stick) butter
⅓ cup brown sugar
⅔ cup honey

Grease two or three cooky sheets and dust lightly with flour.

Sift together the flour, salt, baking soda, ginger, cinnamon and nutmeg. Cream the butter and sugar together until light and fluffy. Beat in the honey, then work in the flour mixture untl a soft dough is formed. Divide in two and wrap in foil or waxed paper; chill 1 hour or until firm enough to roll.

Roll out each piece on a well-floured surface as thin as possible. Cut into any shape or shapes you like. Transfer to the pans with a spatula. Bake in a preheated 350° oven (with oven rack on middle level) 8 minutes or until delicately browned and puffed. Cool on a cake rack.

Makes about 4 dozen.

MERINGUE COCONUT COOKIES

1 cup (6-ounce package)
semi-sweet chocolate chips
2 egg whites
⅛ teaspoon salt
½ cup very fine granulated
sugar

½ teaspoon vinegar
¾ teaspoon vanilla extract
½ cup fine grated coconut
¼ cup chopped pecans or
walnuts

Preheat oven to 350°. Grease two baking sheets.

Melt the chocolate over hot water; cool. Beat the egg whites and salt until foamy. Add 1 tablespoon sugar at a time, beating after each addition. Beat until stiff, then beat in the vinegar and vanilla. Fold in the chocolate, coconut and nuts. Drop by the teaspoon onto the pans, 1 inch apart. Bake 10 minutes. Remove from pans with a spatula.

Makes about 3 dozen.

GREEK PISTACHIO COOKIES

½ pound softened sweet
butter
6 tablespoons sifted
confectioners' sugar
1 egg yolk

2 teaspoons ouzo (a Greek
liquor) or cognac
2¼ cups sifted cake flour
Pistachio nuts

Cream the butter until very soft and fluffy. Beat in the confectioners' sugar, then the egg yolk and *ouzo* or cognac. Work in the flour until a dough is formed. Chill 1 hour.

Break off pieces of the dough and form into balls about 1 inch in diameter. Arrange on cooky sheets and press a pistachio nut into each. Bake in a preheated oven 15 minutes or until pale gold in color. Cool, and sprinkle with confectioners' sugar.

Makes about 3 dozen.

WALNUT SLICES

1¾ cups sifted flour
⅛ teaspoon salt
½ teaspoon baking soda
¼ pound (1 stick) butter

1 cup packed dark brown sugar
1 egg
½ teaspoon vanilla extract
½ cup ground walnuts

Sift together the flour, salt and baking soda.

Cream the butter, then beat in the brown sugar until fluffy. Mix in the egg and vanilla until smooth and fluffy. Add flour mixture to the butter mixture. Work in the nuts. The dough should be very stiff. Form into two rolls 1 inch in diameter. Wrap in foil or waxed paper and chill for 2 hours.

Slice the rolls very thin and arrange on a cooky sheet. Bake on the middle level of a preheated 375° oven 10 minutes.

Makes about 3 dozen.

SPANISH ALMOND DELIGHTS

½ pound (2 sticks) butter
1 cup sugar
3 eggs
2 tablespoons grated lemon rind
2 tablespoons cognac

¼ teaspoon almond extract
1 cup sifted flour
2 cups ground bleached almonds
4 tablespoons heavy cream
¾ cup slivered almonds

Cream the butter, gradually adding the sugar. Beat until fluffy. Add 1 egg at a time, beating well after each addition. Mix in the lemon rind, cognac, almond extract, flour, and ground almonds. Form into a ball; wrap in waxed paper and chill 3 hours.

Roll out the dough on a lightly floured surface as thin as possible. Cut with a floured cooky cutter into any shapes desired. Transfer to a buttered baking sheet with a spatula. Brush with the cream and sprinkle with the slivered almonds. Bake in a preheated 375° oven for 12 minutes, or until delicately browned.

Makes about 4 dozen 3-inch cookies.

BARCELONA ALMOND DROPS

(ROSCAS ALMENDRA)

3 egg whites	rind
4 tablespoons sugar	2 cups ground blanched
2 tablespoons grated lemon	almonds

Preheat oven to 350°.

Beat the egg whites until stiff but not dry. Beat in the sugar gradually, then fold in the rind and almonds. Put through a pastry bag in small twists or drop by the teaspoon onto a greased baking sheet. Bake 10 minutes, or until delicately browned.

Makes about 3 dozen.

ALMOND MERINGUE STRIPS

Batter

4 egg yolks	1 cup ground toasted
1 egg white	almonds
1 cup sugar	2 teaspoons grated lemon
	rind

Preheat oven to 275°. Grease an 8-inch square baking pan and dust with flour.

Beat the egg yolks until thick. Beat the egg whites until peaks form; then gradually beat in the sugar until stiff. Fold into the yolks with the almonds and lemon rind. Turn into the pan. Bake 25 minutes, or until firm when pressed with the fingers. Cool, then turn out onto a baking sheet. Cover with the following meringue.

Meringue

¼ cup water   3 egg whites
¾ cup sugar

Boil the water and sugar until a thread forms when a fork
is lifted from the syrup. Beat the egg whites until stiff, then
gradually beat in the syrup. Cover the top and sides of the
cake, and place in a 275° oven for 10 minutes, or until delicately browned. Cool and cut in strips.

VIENNESE ALMOND CRESCENTS

¾ cup sifted flour   2 teaspoons grated orange
⅛ teaspoon salt   or lemon rind
¼ pound sweet butter   3 tablespoons heavy cream
⅔ cup sugar   ¼ cup ground almonds
4 hard-cooked egg yolks,
   finely mashed

Sift the flour and salt into a bowl. Blend in the butter with
the hand, then ½ cup sugar, the egg yolks and rind, mixing
lightly until a ball of dough is formed. Chill 2 hours. Preheat
the oven to 400°.
Break off small pieces of dough and roll on a lightly floured
surface into 2-inch pencil-slim strips. Work quickly to keep
dough from melting. Arrange on a cooky sheet and turn ends
toward each other to form a crescent. Brush with the cream
and sprinkle with the nuts mixed with the remaining sugar.
Chill 30 minutes. Bake 10 minutes, or until delicately browned.
Cool on a cake rack.

NUT SLICES

2 cups sifted flour   ½ cup firmly packed brown
⅛ teaspoon salt   sugar
1½ teaspoons baking powder   1 egg yolk, beaten
¼ pound (1 stick) butter or   1 tablespoon milk
   margarine   1½ teaspoons vanilla
¾ cup granulated sugar   extract
                                         1 cup chopped nuts

Sift together the flour, salt and baking powder. Cream the butter; beat in the granulated and brown sugars until light and fluffy. Mix in the egg yolk, milk and vanilla, then the nuts. Shape into rolls 1½ inches thick; wrap in aluminum foil or waxed paper. Chill overnight.

With a sharp knife, cut the rolls into slices ⅛ inch thick. Arrange on ungreased baking sheets. Bake in a preheated 400° oven 5 minutes or until delicately browned. The dough can be refrigerated for 2 weeks, so don't bake them all at once if you don't need that many.

Makes about 8 dozen cookies.

CRISP CHOCOLATE NUT COOKIES

½ pound semi-sweet
   chocolate
1 tablespoon brewed coffee
8 egg yolks
⅛ teaspoon salt

½ cup sugar
1 teaspoon vanilla extract
1⅓ cups ground blanched
   almonds
¾ cup flour

Preheat oven to 350°. Grease a cooky sheet and dust lightly with flour.

Break the chocolate into small pieces and combine with the coffee in a saucepan. Place over hot water until melted and smooth. Cool.

Beat the egg yolks, salt and sugar until thick and light. Mix in the vanilla, then the chocolate, nuts and flour. Put through a pastry bag with round tube or drop by the teaspoon onto the cooky sheet, 1 inch apart. Bake 25 minutes or until firm. Cook on a cake rack, and remove with a spatula.

Makes about 3 dozen.

AUSTRIAN NUT CRESCENTS

¼ pound (1 stick) butter
6 tablespoons granulated
   sugar

¾ cup ground walnuts
1⅛ cups sifted flour (about)
Confectioners' sugar

Cream the butter; gradually add the granulated sugar, beating until light and fluffy. Mix in the nuts, then work in just enough of the flour to make a fairly firm dough. Form into a ball, wrap in foil or waxed paper and chill 2 hours.

Break off pieces of the dough and roll it between the palms of the hand into rolls 2 inches long and ½ inch in diameter. Turn ends toward each other to form a crescent and arrange on ungreased cooky sheets. Bake in a preheated 350° oven 15 minutes or until browned around the edges. Cool on a cake rack 10 minutes, then sift confectioners' sugar over them.

Makes about 3 dozen.

CHOCOLATE NUT DROP COOKIES

2 squares (ounces)
   unsweetened chocolate
1½ cups sifted cake flour
½ teaspoon salt
½ teaspoon baking soda
¼ pound (1 stick) butter
1 cup firmly packed brown
   sugar

1 egg, beaten
½ cup milk
1 teaspoon vanilla extract
½ cup chopped walnuts or
   pecans
Mocha Glaze (see recipe)
36 walnut or pecan halves

Preheat oven to 350°. Grease two baking sheets.

Break the chocolate into small pieces; melt over hot water. Cool while preparing the batter. Sift together the flour, salt and baking soda. Cream the butter; gradually beat in the brown sugar until light and fluffy. Mix in the egg and chocolate until smooth. Add the flour mixture alternately with the milk and vanilla, mixing well after each addition. Mix in the chopped nuts. Drop by the heaping teaspoon onto the pans, 2 inches apart. Bake 10 minutes. While still warm, spread with the Mocha Glaze, and place a nut half in the center of each.

Makes about 3 dozen cookies.

Macaroons

ISRAELI ALMOND MACAROONS

1 cup (4½ ounces) ground
  unblanched almonds
¾ cup sugar
1 tablespoon flour

¼ teaspoon salt
2–3 egg whites
¼ teaspoon almond extract
24 blanched almond halves

Preheat oven to 300°. Cover two baking sheets with brown paper or any unglazed paper.

With the hand, mix together the almonds, sugar, flour and salt until thoroughly blended. Beat in 1 egg white at a time, until mixture has the consistency of soft mashed potatoes. It may not be necessary to use the third egg white. Mix in the extract. Force the mixture through a pastry tube or drop by the teaspoonsful, leaving two inches between each. Press an almond half into each.

Bake on the lowest rack 25 minutes or until very delicately browned. Place the papers (macaroons will adhere to it) on a cake rack upside down and place a damp towel on the paper for 5 minutes. Carefully peel the paper from the macaroons. Cool completely, then keep in an air-tight container.

Makes about 24.

COCONUT MACAROONS

¾ cup sweetened condensed
  milk
⅛ teaspoon salt

2 cups (7-ounce package)
  fine-grated coconut
1 teaspoon almond extract

Preheat oven to 325°
Mix all the ingredients together until well-blended. Drop by the teaspoon onto a wet baking sheet, leaving 1 inch between each. Bake 15 minutes or until delicately browned. Remove from pan immediately with a spatula.

Makes about 30.

Variation

Chocolate-Almond Macaroons: Add 2 tablespoons unsweetened cocoa, ½ cup chopped almonds, 2 tablespoons melted butter and an additional 2 tablespoons condensed milk to the coconut macaroon mixture. Proceed as directed.
Makes about 36.

FLORENTINES

4 tablespoons butter	*½ cup blanched almonds,*
¼ cup sugar	*chopped fine*
¼ cup chopped candied	*⅓ cup sifted flour*
orange peel	*3 tablespoons heavy cream*

Preheat oven to 375°.
Cream the butter, then beat in the sugar until light and fluffy. Mix in the orange peel, nuts and flour. Stir in the cream. Drop scant teaspoons of the mixture onto buttered cooky sheets, leaving 2 inches between each. Flatten with a wet fork. Bake 8 minutes, or until browned. Cool 5 minutes, then remove from pan with a spatula.
Makes about 24.

SPANISH CRISPS

¾ cup (1½ sticks) butter	*1½ cups sifted flour*
⅓ cup sugar	*3 tablespoons heavy cream*
1½ teaspoons cinnamon	*¼ cup confectioners' sugar*
3 egg yolks	

Preheat oven to 350°.
Cream the butter, sugar and cinnamon together. Work in the egg yolks and then the flour, until smooth. Chill 30 minutes. Roll out ¼ inch thick and cut into half-moons. Arrange on a cooky sheet; brush with the cream and sprinkle with the confectioners' sugar. Bake 10 minutes, or until browned.
Makes about 4 dozen.

GINGERSNAPS

2¼ cups sifted flour
¾ teaspoon salt
¾ teaspoon baking soda
¼ cup sugar
1½ teaspoons cinnamon

1½ teaspoons ground ginger
⅔ cup shortening
1 cup molasses
2 teaspoons cider vinegar

Sift together the flour, salt, baking soda, sugar, cinnamon and ginger. Blend in the shortening until mixture is like coarse corn meal. Bring the molasses and vinegar to a boil, then stir it into the flour mixture until a dough is formed. Shape into two balls and wrap in foil or waxed paper. Chill overnight or for at least 4 hours. Roll out each ball as thin as possible on a lightly floured surface. Cut into any shape you like with a floured cooky cutter. Arrange on lightly greased baking sheets. Bake in a preheated 400° oven 6 minutes or until edges are delicately browned. Remove from pan immediately with a spatula and let cool on a cake rack.

Makes about 4 dozen 3-inch cookies.

LADYFINGERS

½ cup sifted cake flour
⅛ teaspoon salt
3 egg whites
⅓ cup sifted very fine
   granulated sugar

3 egg yolks
1 tablespoon hot water
1 teaspoon vanilla extract

Preheat oven to 350°. Line a cooky sheet with paper.

Sift the flour and salt 3 times. Beat the egg whites until soft peaks form, then gradually (1 tablespoon at a time) beat in the sugar until very stiff. Beat the egg yolks until thick and light; fold into the egg whites with the water and vanilla. Fold in the flour. Put through a plain-tubed pastry bag onto the paper in 2½-inch lengths, or form into finger lengths with a spoon, leaving ½ inch space between each. Bake 10 minutes or until delicately browned. Cool 2 minutes, then remove from the paper. If they stick, dampen the underside of the paper. Finish cooling. Make sandwiches of the fingers;

brush half the fingers with lightly beaten egg white or jelly and cover with the remaining fingers.
Makes about 24.

FUDGE BROWNIES

2 squares (ounces)
   unsweetened chocolate
¾ cup sifted flour
½ teaspoon salt
1 cup coarsely chopped
   walnuts

⅓ cup butter
1 cup sugar
2 eggs
¾ teaspoon vanilla extract

Preheat oven to 350°. Grease an 8-inch square pan.

Melt the chocolate over hot water. Cool. Sift together the flour and salt; stir in the nuts. Cream the butter; gradually beat in the sugar until light and fluffy. Add 1 egg at a time, beating well after each addition. Mix in the vanilla and chocolate. Stir in the flour mixture until well-blended. Turn into the prepared pan. Bake 30 minutes or until a cake tester comes out clean. Cool on a cake rack and cut into 2-inch squares. These brownies are very moist, and fall slightly when removed from oven. For crisper brownies, add ½ teaspoon baking powder to flour mixture.

Variation

Peppermint Brownies: When brownies are baked, arrange 16 chocolate-covered peppermints on top; return to oven for 3 minutes. Remove from oven and smooth melted peppermints over the top.

BUTTERSCOTCH BROWNIES

1 cup sifted flour
½ teaspoon salt
½ teaspoon baking powder
⅛ teaspoon baking soda
¾ cup coarsely chopped
   walnuts or pecans
⅓ cup butter or margarine

1 cup firmly packed dark
   brown sugar
1 tablespoon hot water
1 egg
1 teaspoon vanilla extract
½ cup caramel or chocolate
   chips

Preheat oven to 350° Grease an 8-inch square baking pan.

Sift together the flour, salt, baking powder and baking soda; Stir in the nuts. Melt the butter in a saucepan. Remove from heat; mix in the brown sugar and water until dissolved. Cool. Beat in the egg and vanilla. Gradually stir in the flour mixture until smooth. Pour into the prepared pan. Sprinkle the caramel chips on top. Bake 20 minutes or until a cake tester comes out clean. Cool on a cake rack. Cut into 2-inch squares.

BUTTERSCOTCH SQUARES

2 cups sifted cake flour
1 teaspoon salt
½ teaspoon baking soda
½ cup butter
1⅓ cups packed brown
    sugar

¾ cup milk
1½ teaspoons vanilla
    extract
2 eggs

Preheat oven to 375°. Grease a 9-inch square pan and dust lightly with flour.

Sift together the flour, salt and baking soda. Cream the butter; sift in the flour mixture. Beat in the brown sugar, add the milk and vanilla, beating very well. Beat in the eggs for 1 minute. Pour into the prepared pan. Bake 35 minutes or until a cake tester comes out clean. Cool on a cake rack for 10 minutes. Turn out and cool completely before frosting with Caramel Frosting. Cut into squares.

COCONUT PECAN SQUARES

1¼ cups sifted cake flour
⅛ teaspoon salt
1¼ cups firmly packed
    brown sugar
⅓ cup melted butter
2 eggs

½ teaspoon double-acting
    baking powder
½ teaspoon almond extract
1¼ cups flaked coconut
1 cup chopped pecans

Preheat oven to 350°.

In a bowl, mix 1 cup flour, the salt and ¼ cup brown sugar. Mix in the butter until smooth. Press on the bottom of an 8-inch square baking. pan. Bake 15 minutes.

Prepare the topping during this time. Beat the eggs until thick; gradually beat in the remaining brown sugar until light and fluffy. Sift the baking powder and remaining flour into the mixture; stir until smooth. Mix in the almond extract, coconut and nuts. Remove pan from oven and quickly spread coconut mixture over the pastry. Return to oven and bake 20 minutes longer or until delicately browned. Cut into 2-inch squares while warm.

CHOCOLATE BALLS

3 squares (ounces) unsweetened chocolate	*1 cup ground walnuts or pecans*
1 tablespoon brewed coffee	*1 tablespoon rum*
½ pound (2 sticks) butter	*2½ cups sifted flour*
¼ cup sugar	*Sugar for rolling*
1 egg yolk	*Walnut or pecan halves*

Break the chocolate into small pieces and combine with the coffee in a small saucepan. Place over hot water until melted and smooth. Cool.

Cream the butter and sugar until light and fluffy. Beat in the egg yolk, nuts, rum and chocolate, then mix in the flour. Chill 1 hour.

Form teaspoons of the dough into balls, roll in sugar and arrange on greased cooky sheets, leaving space between each. Lightly press a nut half into each ball. Bake in a preheated 325° oven 15 minutes or until dry. Cool on a cake rack.

Makes about 4 dozen.

CHOCOLATE DATE-NUT BARS

1 cup finely chopped dates	*1 cup sugar*
1 cup boiling water	*2 eggs*
1 teaspoon baking soda	*1 teaspoon vanilla extract*
1¾ cups sifted flour	*1 cup semi-sweet chocolate chips*
¼ cup unsweetened cocoa	*½ cup chopped pecans or walnuts*
½ teaspoon salt	
1 cup shortening	

Preheat oven to 350°. Grease a 10-by-15-inch jelly roll pan. Combine the dates, boiling water and baking soda. Let stand until cool. Sift together the flour, cocoa and salt.

Cream the shortening. Gradually beat in the sugar until light and fluffy. Beat in 1 egg at a time, then the vanilla. Add the flour mixture alternately with the date mixture, beating well after each addition. Spread in the prepared pan. Arrange the chocolate chips and nuts over it. Bake 30 minutes. Cool on a cake rack; cut into 36 bars while still warm.

POLISH ALMOND BARS

(MAZURKA)

½ pound (2 sticks) butter
1 cup sugar
5 hard-cooked egg yolks, mashed
½ teaspoon vanilla extract
⅛ teaspoon salt

2¼ cups sifted flour
1 egg white
1 teaspoon water
1½ cups sliced blanched almonds

Grease an 8-inch square shallow baking pan. Place oven rack on middle level.

Cream the butter and sugar together until light and fluffy. Blend in the mashed egg yolks, vanilla and salt. Stir in the flour until smooth. Pat the dough into the pan. Chill 2 hours.

Brush the top of the dough with the egg white mixed with the water. Sprinkle the almonds over it. Bake in a preheated 350° oven 40 minutes or until delicately browned and firm. Cool 5 minutes, then with a sharp knife cut into bars 1 inch wide and 2 inches long.

DUTCH POPPY SEED BARS

2½ sticks (1¼ cups) butter
1 cup sugar
¼ teaspoon almond extract
1½ cups ground almonds
3 cups sifted flour

½ teaspoon ginger
¼ teaspoon mace
1 egg, beaten
¾ cup poppy seeds

Grease an 11-by-16-inch jelly roll pan.

Cream the butter an dsugar until light and fluffy. Blend in the almond extract and almonds, then the flour mixed with the ginger and mace. Pat into the pan. Chill 2 hours. Brush top with the egg and sprinkle with the poppy seeds, pressing them down lightly with the hand. Bake in a preheated 375° oven (with oven rack on middle level) 20 minutes or until delicately browned. Cool 5 minutes, then with a sharp knife cut into bars 1 inch wide and 2 inches long.

COCONUT SHORTBREAD

1½ cups sifted flour	½ pound (2 sticks) softened
¼ cup cornstarch	butter
¾ cup sifted confectioners'	1 teaspoon vanilla extract
sugar	2 cups fine grated coconut

Sift together the flour, cornstarch and confectioners' sugar. Blend in the butter and vanilla with the hand until a dough is formed. Chill 1 hour.

Break off small pieces of the dough and shape into walnut-sized balls. Roll in the coconut. Arrange on ungreased baking sheets, leaving 1 inch between each. Bake in a preheated 300° oven 20 minutes or until delicately browned. Remove from pan with a spatula.

Makes about 4 dozen cookies.

SCOTCH SHORTBREAD

¾ cup (1½ sticks) sweet	1¾ cups sifted flour
butter	½ teaspoon salt
⅔ cup confectioners' sugar	

Preheat the oven to 325°.

Cream the butter; beat in the sugar gradually until very light and fluffy. Sift flour and salt over it and work in with the hand until thoroughly blended. Pat into the bottom of an 11-inch pie plate. Using a fluted pastry cutter or sharp knife, cut about halfway through the dough into 24 wedges, then prick the top with the tines of a fork. Bake on the middle rack 45 minutes, or until pale yellow and firm to the touch in the center. Cool on a cake rack, then turn out, top side up onto a board. Cut through the wedges where marked.

ITALIAN CRULLERS

(SFINGE)

2 cups sifted flour	½ cup sugar
¼ teaspoon salt	1 tablespoon vegetable oil
3 teaspoons baking powder	⅓ cup milk
½ teaspoon mace	Fat for deep frying
2 eggs	Powdered sugar

Sift together the flour, salt, baking powder and mace. Beat the eggs, sugar and oil until thick. Stir in the milk, then the flour mixture. Beat until very smooth. Cover with a towel and let stand 15 minutes.

Heat the fat to 370°. Drop the batter into it by the tablespoon, a few at a time. Fry until browned, about 4 minutes. Remove with a slotted spoon and drain. Sprinkle with sugar, anise-flavored if you like.

Makes about 3 dozen.

Pies

BLUEBERRY PIE

2 12-ounce packages frozen
  blueberries, thawed
¼ cup minute tapioca
⅓ cup sugar
¼ teaspoon salt

¼ teaspoon cinnamon
1 tablespoon lemon juice
Pastry for 2-crust 9-inch pies
1 tablespoon butter

Preheat oven to 425°.

Drain the berries well, reserving ½ cup juice. Combine the reserved juice, berries, tapioca, sugar, salt, cinnamon and lemon juice. Let stand 15 minutes. Roll out a little more than half the pastry as thin as possible; line a 9-inch pie plate with it. Fill the shell with the berry mixture. Dot with the butter. Roll out the remaining pastry, cut a few slits in the top and fit over the fruit, sealing the edges well. Bake 50 minutes or until browned. Cool on a cake rack.

BERRY PIE

Pastry for 2-crust pie
4 cups blueberries, rasp-
  berries, strawberries or
  blackberries, washed and
  drained

1 tablespoon cornstarch
¾ cup sugar
⅛ teaspoon salt
2 teaspoons lemon juice

Preheat oven to 425°. Line a 9-inch pie plate with a little more than half the pastry.

Lightly toss together the berries, the cornstarch, sugar, salt and lemon juice. Fill the lined pie plate. Roll out the remaining pastry and cut a few slits in the top. Cover the fruit, sealing the edges well. For a glossy crust, brush with cream or beaten egg yolk. Bake 45 minutes or until browned. Cool on a cake rack.

FRESH RED CHERRY PIE

4 cups fresh pitted sour red
 cherries
2 tablespoons cornstarch

1¼ cups sugar
Pastry for 2-crust pie

Preheat oven to 400°.

Combine the cherries, cornstarch and sugar in a saucepan; cook over low heat, stirring constantly to the boiling point. Cook 5 minutes longer, stirring occasionally. Cool. Line a 9-inch pie plate with a little more than half the pastry. Fill with the cherries. Roll out remaining pastry, cut a few slits in the top and cover the fruit, sealing the edges well. Or cut the pastry into strips and form into a lattice covering. Bake 45 minutes or until browned. Cool on a cake rack.

CANNED RED CHERRY PIE

1 #2 can pitted sour
 cherries
2 tablespoons minute
 tapioca

¾ cup sugar
Dash salt
⅛ teaspoon almond extract
Pastry for 2-crust pie

Preheat oven to 400°.

Drain the cherries, reserving 1 cup juice. Combine the cherries, reserved juice, tapioca, sugar, salt and almond extract. Let stand 15 minutes. Line a 9-inch pie plate with a little more than half the pastry. Fill with the cherry mixture. Cover with remaining pastry, sealing the edges well. Cut a few slits in the top. Bake 45 minutes or until browned. Cool on a cake rack.

APPLE PIE

Pastry for 2-crust pie
6 cups thinly sliced tart
 apples, peeled
¾ cup sugar

1 teaspoon cinnamon or
 nutmeg
2 tablespoons butter or
 margarine

Preheat oven to 425°. Line a 9-inch pie plate with a little more than half the pastry.

Toss together the apples, sugar and cinnamon. Fill the prepared pie plate. Dot with the butter. Roll out the remaining pastry, cut slits in it and cover the apples, sealing the edges well. For a glossy crust, brush with cream or beaten egg. Bake 45 minutes or until browned.

Apple-Cheese Pie: Prepare the cheese pastry, and proceed as directed above, omitting the cinnamon or nutmeg.

APPLE CUSTARD PIE

4 teaspoons cornstarch
⅛ teaspoon salt
1 cup sugar
2 eggs, beaten
½ cup heavy cream, whipped
2 cups chopped apples

1 9-inch unbaked pastry shell
4 tablespoons butter
¼ cup sifted flour
¾ teaspoon cinnamon
⅛ teaspoon nutmeg

Preheat oven to 450°.

Sift together the cornstarch, salt and ¾ cup sugar. Beat in the eggs until smooth, then stir in the whipped cream and apples. Spread in the pie shell. Bake 10 minutes, reduce heat to 350° and bake 20 minutes longer. While the pie is baking, mix together the butter, flour, cinnamon, nutmeg and remaining sugar until the consistency of crumbs. Spread over the pie and bake 10 minutes longer, or until browned. Cool.

COCONUT CUSTARD PIE

4 eggs
¼ teaspoon salt
⅓ cup sugar
2 cups milk

1 cup light cream
1 teaspoon vanilla extract
1¼ cups fine-grated coconut
1 unbaked 9-inch pie shell

Preheat oven to 425°.

Beat together the eggs, slat and sugar. Stir in the milk, cream and vanilla, then the coconut. Pour into the lined pie plate. Bake 30 minutes, or until a knife inserted in the center comes out clean. Cool on a cake rack.

FRUIT CUSTARD-MERINGUE PIE

Filling

Pastry for 1-crust pie
2 cups peeled sliced apples
  or peaches
3 egg yolks

⅛ teaspoon salt
⅔ cup sugar
2 cups milk
½ teaspoon vanilla extract

Preheat oven to 450°. Line a 9-inch pie plate with the pastry. Chill 10 minutes.

Arrange the fruit on the bottom of the lined pie plate. Beat the egg yolks, salt and sugar until light and fluffy. Mix in the milk and vanilla; pour over the fruit. Bake 10 minutes; reduce heat to 325° and bake 30 minutes longer or until a knife inserted in the center comes out clean. Cool.

Meringue

3 egg whites
⅓ cup sugar

3 tablespoons finely chopped
  nuts

Beat the egg whites until soft peaks are formed, then gradually beat in the sugar until stiff. Fold in the nuts. Spread over the pie, covering the edges. Bake in a preheated 425° oven 5 minutes or until delicately browned. Cool.

ORANGE-CUSTARD PIE

4 eggs
¾ cup sugar
1½ cups light cream, scalded
2 teaspoons grated orange
  rind
1⅔ cups orange juice

1 9-inch unbaked pie shell
2 oranges, peeled, seeded
  and sectioned
1½ teaspoons cornstarch
3 tablespoons Orange
  Liqueur (Curaçao)

Preheat oven to 425°.

Beat the eggs and sugar until light and fluffy; gradually beat in the cream. Mix in the orange rind and 1⅓ cups orange juice. Pour into the lined pie plate. Bake 35 minutes or until a knife inserted in the center comes out clean. Arrange the orange sections on top.

In a small saucepan, mix together the cornstarch and remaining orange juice. Cook over low heat, stirring steadily until thick and clear. Add the liqueur. Spoon evenly over the oranges. Chill.

BANANA PIE

Pastry for 2-crust pie
6 bananas
½ cup sugar
1 tablespoon melted butter
½ cup ground almonds

1 cup chopped seedless
raisins
1 teaspoon cinnamon
¼ teaspoon nutmeg
½ teaspoon powdered ginger
3 egg whites, stiffly beaten

Preheat oven to 425°.
Line a 9-inch pie plate with a little more than half the pastry. Chill while preparing the filling.
Mash the bananas very smooth. Stir in the sugar, butter, almonds, raisins, cinnamon, nutmeg, and ginger. Fold in the egg whites. Turn the banana mixture into the lined pie plate. Cover with the remaining rolled-out pastry. Bake 35 minutes, or until browned. Cool on a cake rack.
Serves 6–8.

LEMON-CURD MERINGUE PIE

3 eggs
1⅛ cups sugar
⅓ cup lemon juice
6 tablespoons butter

1 tablespoon grated lemon
rind
Baked 9-inch pastry shell
3 egg whites

Preheat oven to 400°.
Beat the eggs and ⅞ cup of the sugar in the top of a double boiler. Stir in the lemon juice and add the butter, broken in small pieces. Place over hot water and cook, stirring steadily until thickened and mixture coats the spoon. Stir in the lemon rind and let cool. Pour into the pie plate.
Beat the egg whites until peaks form, then beat in the remaining sugar, a tablespoon at a time, until stiff but not dry. Heap on the lemon filling (using a pastry tube, if you like). Bake 5 minutes or until meringue is delicately browned. Cool.

LEMON SPONGE PIE

1¼ cups crushed vanilla
    wafers
3 tablespoons melted butter
¼ pound (1 stick) butter
¾ cup sugar
2 tablespoons cornstarch

3 egg yolks
1 cup milk
3 tablespoons lemon juice
2 teaspoons grated lemon
    rind
3 egg whites, stiffly beaten

Preheat oven to 350°.

Mix the vanilla wafers and melted butter together. Line a 9-inch buttered pie plate with the mixture. Chill while preparing the filling.

Cream the ¼ pound butter, gradually adding the sugar and cornstarch. Beat until light and fluffy. Add 1 egg yolk at a time, beating after each addition. Add the milk, lemon juice and rind, beating very well. Fold in the egg whites carefully but thoroughly. Pour into prepared pie plate. Bake 35 minutes, or until delicately browned.

LEMON CHIFFON PIE

1 envelope (tablespoon)
    gelatin
¼ cup cold water
4 egg yolks
1 cup sugar
½ cup lemon juice

1 teaspoon grated lemon
    rind
2 egg whites
⅛ teaspoon salt
½ cup heavy cream
9-inch baked pastry or
    crumb shell

Soften the gelatin in the water. Beat the egg yolks in the top of a double boiler; mix in ½ cup sugar and the lemon juice. Place over hot water and cook, stirring steadily, until mixture coats the spoon. Mix in the gelatin until dissolved, then the rind. Remove from the hot water and let cool, mixing occasionally.

Beat the egg whites and salt until they begin to stiffen, then gradually beat in the remaining sugar until stiff. Whip the cream. Fold in the lemon mixture, then the beaten egg whites. Turn into the prepared pie shell. Chill until set. Decorate with whipped cream if you like.

Variation

Lime Chiffon Pie: Substitute lime juice and rind for the lemon and add 2 drops of green food coloring.

MOCHA CHIFFON PIE

1 envelope (tablespoon) gelatin	¼ teaspoon salt
¼ cup cold water	2 egg yolks
1 cup milk	½ cup heavy cream
1 cup semi-sweet chocolate chips	2 egg whites
1 tablespoon instant coffee	3 tablespoons sugar
	9-inch baked baked pastry or crumb shell

Soften the gelatin in the water. In a saucepan, combine the milk, chocolate, coffee and salt. Cook over low heat, stirring steadily, until chocolate melts. Beat the egg yolks in a bowl; very gradually add the chocolate mixture, stirring steadily to prevent curdling. Return to the saucepan and cook, stirring steadily until thickened. Do not let boil. Remove from the heat and stir in the gelatin until dissolved. Cool. Whip the cream. Beat the egg whites until foamy; gradually beat in the sugar until stiff. Fold into the chocolate mixture with the whipped cream. Turn into the pie shell. Chill until firm. Decorate with whipped cream and shaved chocolate, if desired.

ITALIAN FRUIT-ALMOND PIE

Pastry

1¼ cups flour	¼ pound (1 stick) butter or margarine
½ teaspoon salt	2 egg yolks
1 teaspoon baking powder	2 tablespoons Marsala or sweet sherry
¼ cup sugar	
½ teaspoon cinnamon	
2 teaspoons grated lemon rind	

Sift the flour, salt, baking powder, sugar, cinnamon and lemon rind into a bowl. Cut in the butter with a pastry blender or 2 knives. Beat the egg yolks and wine; stir into the flour mixture with a fork until all the particles hold together. Roll out on a lightly floured surface to fit an 11-inch pie plate. Fit the dough into the greased pie plate. Chill while preparing the filling.

Filling

5 cups sliced apples	½ cup ground almonds
2 tablespoons cognac	½ teaspoon cinnamon
¾ cup sugar	¼ teaspoon mace
2 tablespoons flour	

Toss the apples with the cognac; arrange in the lined pie plate. Mix together the sugar, flour, nuts, cinnamon and mace; sprinkle over the apples. Bake in a preheated 375° oven 45 minutes, or until apples are tender. Serve warm or cold, cut into wedges.

BOSTON CREAM PIE

Cake

1¾ cups sifted cake flour	1 teaspoon vanilla extract
¼ teaspoon salt	2 egg yolks
2 teaspoons baking powder	½ cup milk
6 tablespoons butter	2 egg whites, beaten stiff
1 cup sugar	

Preheat oven to 375°.

Sift together the flour, salt and baking powder. Cream the butter; gradually beat in the sugar until very fluffy. Beat in the vanilla, then 1 egg yolk at a time. Add the flour and milk alternately, stirring only until blended. Start and end with the flour. Fold in the egg whites, carefully but thoroughly. Turn into a greased 9-inch pie plate. Bake 35 minutes, or until a cake tester comes out clean. Cool on a cake rack 10 minutes, then remove from the pie plate. Turn right side. With a sharp knife, cut out about a 7-inch circle almost down to the bottom.

Lift up carefully. Fill the cake, and replace top. Cover with Chocolate Glaze.

Filling

½ cup flour
⅔ cup sugar
⅛ teaspoon salt
2 cups milk, scalded

2 egg yolks
1 teaspoon vanilla extract
1 cup whipped cream

Sift the flour, sugar and salt into the top of a double boiler. Stir in the hot milk gradually. Place over hot water and cook, stirring constantly, until thickened. Cook 5 minutes longer.

Beat the egg yolks in a bowl; gradually add the hot mixture, stirring steadily to prevent curdling. Return to the double boiler and cook 2 minutes, stirring steadily. Cool. Stir in the vanilla and fold in the whipped cream.

PUMPKIN PIE

Pastry for 1-crust pie
2 cups cooked or canned
   pumpkin
½ teaspoon salt
⅔ cup firmly packed brown
   sugar
1 teaspoon cinnamon

½ teaspoon ground ginger
½ teaspoon nutmeg
2 eggs, beaten
1 cup milk
1 cup light cream
2 tablespoons cognac

Preheat oven to 325°. Line a 9-inch pie plate with the pastry and chill while preparing the filling.

Using an electric blender, electric mixer or rotary beater, beat together the pumpkin, salt, brown sugar, cinnamon, ginger, nutmeg and eggs until smooth, then gradually add the milk, cream and cognac. Pour into the lined pie plate. Bake 50 minutes or until a knife inserted in the center comes out clean. Serve warm, with whipped cream, if desired.

FROZEN EGGNOG PIE

1½ cups graham cracker
    crumbs
⅓ cup ground unblanched
    almonds
⅓ cup confectioners' sugar
¼ cup light cream
½ cup melted butter
1 envelope (tablespoon)
    gelatin

1 cup milk
¾ cup granulated sugar
¼ teaspoon salt
4 egg yolks
2 tablespoons cognac or
    light rum
4 egg whites
¼ cup sliced candied
    cherries

Preheat the oven to 375°.

Mix together the cracker crumbs, almonds, confectioners' sugar, cream and butter. Press the mixture into a 9-inch pie plate. Bake 15 minutes. Cool and chill.

Soften the gelatin in the milk in the top of a double boiler. Add ¼ cup of the granulated sugar, the salt and egg yolks. Beat until blended. Place over hot water and cook, stirring constantly until thickened and the mixture coats the back of the spoon. Remove from the heat, mix in the cognac and chill until thickened but not firm.

Beat the egg whites until foamy. Gradually add the remaining half cup of sugar, beating until stiff but not dry. Fold the meringue and the cherries into the gelatin mixture. Pile in the crumb shell. Cover with clear plastic wrap supported above the filling on four to six toothpicks stuck into the pie. Freeze, then wrap in foil. To serve the pie, thaw it at room temperature one hour. Decorate with whipped cream and cherries, if desired.

Makes 6 servings.

BLACK BOTTOM PIE

2 cups gingersnap crumbs
½ cup (¼ pound) melted
  butter
1 envelope (tablespoon)
  gelatin
¼ cup cold water
4 egg yolks
1½ tablespoons cornstarch
¾ cup sugar

2 cups milk, scalded
2 squares (ounces) un-
  sweetened chocolate,
  melted
1 teaspoon vanilla extract
3 tablespoons rum
4 egg whites
1 cup heavy cream
Shaved chocolate

Preheat oven to 350°.

Mix the crumbs and melted butter together. Press onto the sides and bottom of an 11-inch buttered pie plate. Bake 10 minutes; cool.

Soften the gelatin in the water. In the top of a double boiler, beat the egg yolks, cornstarch and ½ cup sugar; gradually add the hot milk, mixing steadily. Place over hot water and cook, mixing steadily until mixture coats the spoon. Remove from heat and pour half the mixture into a bowl; mix in the chocolate and vanilla. Cool, then pour into the pie shell. To mixture remaining in the double boiler, add the gelatin and rum, stirring until gelatin dissolves. Cool. Beat the egg whites until soft peaks are formed; gradually beat in the remaining sugar until stiff. Whip the cream and fold half into the gelatin mixture with the beaten egg whites. Pour into the pie plate. Chill. Cover top with the remaining whipped cream and shaved chocolate.

BLACK WALNUT PIE

2 tablespoons flour
¼ cup sugar
2 eggs
1 cup dark corn syrup
½ cup water

1 cup (¼ pound) black
  walnuts
1 unbaked 9-inch pastry
  shell

Preheat the oven to 375°.

Mix the flour and sugar. Beat the eggs, then beat in the sugar mixture until blended. Stir in the corn syrup and water. Mix in the nuts. Pour into pastry shell. Bake 35 minutes or until a knife inserted in the center comes out clean.

PECAN PIE

Pastry for 1-crust pie
4 tablespoons butter
⅔ cup firmly packed dark
   brown sugar

¾ cup dark corn syrup
3 eggs
1 teaspoon vanilla extract
1 cup pecan halves

Preheat oven to 400°. Line an 8-inch pie plate with the pastry; chill while preparing the filling.

Cream the butter, gradually beating in the brown sugar until light and fluffy. Beat in the corn syrup, then 1 egg at a time. Mix in the vanilla and pecans. Turn into the lined pie plate. Bake 10 minutes; reduce heat to 350° and bake 30 minutes longer or until a knife inserted in the center comes out clean. Cool. Serve with whipped cream, if desired.

CHEESE PIE

1 pound cream cheese
¾ cup sugar
2 eggs
2 tablespoons heavy cream
2 teaspoons vanilla extract

9-inch pie plate, lined with
   pastry dough or graham
   cracker pastry
½ cup sour cream

Preheat oven to 350°.

Using an electric mixer or rotary beater, beat the cheese until smooth. Add all but 2 tablespoons sugar; beat until light and fluffy. Beat in the eggs, cream and 1 teaspoon vanilla. Turn into the lined pie plate. Bake 20 minutes.

Mix together the sour cream and remaining vanilla and sugar. Spread over the top of the pie at the end of 20 minutes' baking time. Raise heat to 425° and bake 5 minutes longer. Cool, then chill several hours before serving.

CRUSTLESS FUDGE PIE

2 squares (ounces) un-
  sweetened chocolate
2 tablespoons brewed coffee
¼ pound (1 stick) butter or
  margarine
1 cup sugar

⅛ teaspoon salt
1 teaspoon vanilla
2 egg yolks
⅓ cup sifted flour
2 egg whites, stiffly beaten

Preheat oven to 350°.

Melt the chocolate in the coffee; cool. Cream the butter, gradually adding the sugar. Beat until light and fluffy. Add the salt, vanilla, and 1 egg yolk at a time. Add the flour and chocolate, mixing thoroughly. Fold in the egg whites carefully.

Pour into a buttered 9-inch pie plate. Bake 45 minutes, or until set and puffed. Cool and serve with whipped cream. Cut like a pie.

VANILLA CREAM PIE

⅔ cup sugar
½ teaspoon salt
3 tablespoons cornstarch
2½ cups milk
3 egg yolks

2 tablespoons butter or
  margarine
2 teaspoons vanilla extract
1 9-inch baked pastry or
  crumb shell

In the top of a double boiler, mix the sugar, salt and cornstarch. Stir in the milk. Cook over low heat, stirring constantly to the boiling point, then cook 3 minutes longer. Beat the egg yolks in a bowl; gradually add the hot mixture, stirring steadily to prevent curdling. Return to the double boiler and place over boiling water. Cook 10 minutes, stirring frequently. Remove from the heat and stir in the butter and vanilla until butter melts. Cool. Pour into the pie shell and chill. Cover with whipped cream and shaved chocolate if desired.

Variation

Chocolate Cream Pie: Add 2 squares (ounces) melted semi-sweet chocolate to the mixture when adding the butter.

COCONUT MERINGUE-SHELL PIE

¼ pound sweet chocolate
3 tablespoons brewed coffee
2 egg yolks, beaten
1 cup heavy cream

1 tablespoon confectioners'
  sugar
1 9-inch baked Coconut
  Meringue Shell

Break the chocolate into small pieces; combine with the coffee in a small saucepan. Place over hot water until melted; stir until smooth. Cool 5 minutes. Gradually add the egg yolks, stirring constantly to prevent curdling. Return to the hot water and cook 1 minute, mixing steadily. Cool. Whip the cream and confectioners' sugar. Fold half into the chocolate mixture. Spread remaining whipped cream on the bottom of the pie shell. Cover with the chocolate mixture. Chill at least 4 hours. Decorate with whipped cream, if desired.

SWEET POTATO-NUT PIE

Pastry for 1-crust pie
4 eggs
½ teaspoon salt
½ cup sugar
1½ cups mashed sweet
  potatoes
2 tablespoons honey

⅔ cup milk
⅓ cup orange juice
1 teaspoon vanilla extract
¼ teaspoon nutmeg
½ cup chopped walnuts or
  pecans

Preheat oven to 375°. Line a 9-inch pie plate with the pastry and chill while preparing the filling.

Beat the eggs and salt, then beat in the sugar. Beat in the sweet potatoes and honey until smooth. Add the milk, orange juice, vanilla and nutmeg, beating again until smooth. Stir in the nuts. Pour into the lined pie plate. Bake 40 minutes or until a knife inserted in the center comes out clean. Serve warm, with whipped cream if desired.

Pastry

FLAKY PASTRY

2 cups sifted flour
¾ teaspoon salt

¾ cup shortening
6 tablespoons ice water

Sift the flour and salt into a bowl. Using a pastry blender or two knives, cut in ½ cup of the shortening until the consistency of coarse corn meal. Break up the remaining shortening and cut in until mixture is the size of peas. Sprinkle with a little water and toss with a fork, adding just enough water to make the flour mixture cling together. Wrap in a damp cloth and chill 30 minutes.

Divide dough in two, making one piece slightly larger than the other. On a lightly floured surface, roll out the larger piece as thin as possible. Fit into an ungreased 9-inch pie plate. Trim the edges. Brush edges with water or egg white. Fill with selected filling. Roll out the remaining pastry as thin as possible. Cut a few slits in the top. Cover the filling with the pastry. Press edges together on the rim to seal; fold edge of top crust under bottom and flute or press with the tines of a fork. Bake as directed for each recipe.

Variation

Cheese Pastry: Add ½ cup Cheddar Cheese with the remaining shortening. Proceed as directed.

FRENCH TART PASTE

(PÂTÉ SUCRÉE)

1 cup sifted flour
⅛ teaspoon salt
1 tablespoon sugar

¼ pound (1 stick) sweet butter (at room temperature)
1 egg yolk
1 tablespoon ice water

Sift the flour, salt and sugar into a bowl; make a well in the center. Place the butter, egg yolk and water in the well; work in the flour with the hand until a ball of dough is formed. Chill 2 hours or overnight. Roll out ⅛ inch thick on a lightly floured surface and fit into a buttered 9-inch pie plate or *flan* ring. (A metal ring with straight sides and no bottom. The ring is placed on a buttered baking sheet.) Flute the edges and chill 30 minutes before filling. To prebake the shell, prick the bottom in several places with a fork and place a pie plate or waxed paper covered with rice or beans over it to keep from shrinking. Bake in a preheated 400° oven 20 minutes or until browned. Remove the weight and cool.

SOUR CREAM PASTRY

2 cups sifted flour
¼ teaspoon salt

½ pound (2 sticks) butter
 or margarine
6 tablespoons sour cream

Sift the flour and salt into a bowl. With a pastry blender or two knives, cut in the butter until mixture forms pieces the size of peas. Blend in the sour cream until a ball of dough is formed. Wrap in foil or waxed paper; chill overnight or at least 2 hours. Roll out and proceed as directed for each recipe.

Makes enough for a 2-crust 9-inch pie.

WALNUT PASTRY

1¼ cups sifted flour
⅛ teaspoon salt
¾ cup finely ground
 walnuts

¼ pound (1 stick) butter or
 margarine
4 tablespoons ice water

Sift the flour and salt into bowl; mix in the walnuts. Using a pastry blender or 2 knives, cut in the butter until mixture is like coarse corn meal. Gradually add the water, tossing lightly until particles stick together. (It may not be necessary to add all the water.) Form into a ball and chill 2 hours before rolling. Proceed as directed in each recipe.

Makes enough for a 2-crust 9-inch pie.

MERINGUE PASTRY SHELL, PARIS STYLE

3 egg whites
⅛ teaspoon salt
¼ teaspoon cream of tartar

¾ cup very fine granulated
   sugar
1 teaspoon vanilla extract

Preheat oven to 300°.

Have the egg whites at room temperature. Beat the egg whites and salt until foamy. Add the cream of tartar and beat until soft peaks are formed. Add 2 tablespoons of sugar at a time, beating until very stiff. Beat in the vanilla. Spread the meringue over the bottom and sides of a 9-inch pie plate, piling it about 1 inch above the edge of the plate. Bake 45 minutes or until delicately browned and dry. Carefully loosen the shell from the pan while warm, but leave in pie plate. Cool thoroughly before filling. Use with any filling which does not require baking.

Variation

Coconut Meringue Shell: Toss ⅔ cup fine-grated coconut with 3 tablespoons sifted confectioners' sugar, to coat coconut. Fold into the meringue and proceed as directed.

GRAHAM CRACKER PASTRY SHELL

1¼ cups fine graham
     cracker crumbs
2 tablespoons sugar

⅓ cup melted cooled butter
   or margarine

Mix all the ingredients together. Press firmly on the bottom and sides of a 9-inch pie plate. Bake in a preheated 375° oven 6 minutes; cool before filling. For unbaked shell, chill 1 hour before filling.

Variation

GINGERSNAP CRUMB PASTRY SHELL

1¼ cups fine gingersnap   ¼ cup melted cooled butter
      crumbs   or margarine
3 tablespoons sugar

Proceed as directed for Graham Cracker Pastry Shell.

CHOCOLATE CRUMB PASTRY SHELL

1¼ cups chocolate cooky   ¼ cup melted cooled butter
      crumbs   or margarine
2 tablespoons sugar

Proceed as directed for Graham Cracker Pastry Shell.

ZWIEBACK PASTRY SHELL

1¼ cups fine zwieback   ⅓ cup melted cooled butter
      crumbs   or margarine
2 tablespoons sugar

Proceed as directed for Graham Cracker Pastry Shell.

HUNGARIAN STRUDEL

Dough

2½ cups flour   ½ cup vegetable oil
½ teaspoon salt   2 egg whites
2 teaspoons vinegar   ½ cup warm water

Sift the flour and salt together into a bowl. Make a well in
the center. Into it put the vinegar, ¼ cup oil and egg whites.
Gradually work in the flour, adding just enough of the warm

water to make a soft dough. It may not be necessary to add all the water. Knead well; raise the dough and slap it down several times until it loses its stickiness. This will take 10–15 minutes. Form into a ball, brush with oil, and cover with a warm bowl for 30 minutes.

Spread a cloth over a large table and dust with flour. Roll out the dough in a circle, turning it several times. Brush with oil. Flour both hands heavily and begin stretching the dough from underneath with the backs of the hands. Work carefully and brush with more oil occasionally. Don't worry if the dough tears; it should be almost transparent. Cut off the thick edges. Let dry for 5 minutes.

Cheese Filling

¼ pound (1 stick) butter
¾ cup sugar
6 egg yolks
1¾ cups sour cream
2 teaspoons grated lemon
   rind

1 pound cream cheese
½ cup seedless raisins
   (optional)
6 egg whites, beaten stiff

Melt half the butter and brush the dough with it.

Cream the remaining butter; gradually adding the sugar. Add the egg yolks, beating until light and fluffy. Add the sour cream and lemon rind. Force the cheese through a sieve. Combine with previous mixture, beating until thoroughly smooth. Add the raisins, if desired. Fold in the egg whites. Spread the cheese mixture over two-thirds of the dough. Turn opposite sides in and roll up loosely. Brush with melted butter. Place on a buttered baking sheet. Bake in a preheated 375° oven 45 minutes, or until delicately browned. Cut into 2-inch slices while hot.

Apple Filling

3 tablespoons butter
1½ cups fresh bread crumbs
¾ cup melted butter
¾ cup ground walnuts
4 cups peeled sliced apples

1 cup seedless raisins
   (optional)
2 teaspoons grated lemon
   rind
⅔ cup sugar
1 tablespoon cinnamon

Melt the 3 tablespoons butter in a skillet; sauté the bread crumbs in it until lightly browned. Cool.

Brush the strudel dough generously with melted butter. Sprinkle with the bread crumbs and walnuts. Spread the apples in a 2-inch strip along one end of the dough. Brush with melted butter and sprinkle with the raisins, lemon rind, sugar and cinnamon. Fold in opposite sides of the dough. Starting from the apple end, lift up the cloth, and roll up like a jelly roll. Transfer the roll to a greased baking sheet. (If roll is too long for the pan, turn ends in.) Brush with melted butter. Bake in a preheated 350° oven 50 minutes or until delicately browned. Brush with melted butter a few times during the baking period. Sprinkle top with sugar. Serve warm, cut into 2-inch pieces.

Poppy Seed Filling

½ pound poppy seeds
¼ pound (1 stick) butter
½ cup honey
1½ cups coarsely chopped
  walnuts or pecans

½ cup seedless raisins
¼ cup heavy cream
1 tablespoon grated orange
  rind

Have the poppy seeds ground where you buy them, or cover with boiling water and let soak 2 hours, then drain well and grind twice, using the finest blade of the meat chopper.

Cream the butter; beat in the honey, nuts, raisins, cream and orange rind. Proceed as directed.

FRENCH PUFF PASTE

(PÂTÉ FEUILLETÉE)

4 cups sifted flour
1¼ cups ice water (about)
1 teaspoon salt

1 tablespoon lemon juice
1 pound (4 sticks) sweet
  butter

Sift the flour onto a board and make a well in the center. Pour 1 cup ice water, the salt and lemon juice into it and work in the flour, until a firm dough is formed. If too dry, add a little more water. Knead and pound dough until smooth and elastic. Cover with a bowl for 10 minutes. Roll out into a rectangle about 10 by 18 inches. Shape the butter into a square and place it in the center. Fold the dough over the butter, wrap in a napkin and chill 15 minutes. Roll into a long strip, being careful not to let the butter break through. Fold in thirds, open edges towards you. Roll and fold again. Chill for 30 minutes. Repeat the process three times, always keeping the open edges out, and never exposing the butter. Chill for at least two hours before using as directed in recipes using puff paste.

NAPOLEONS

(MILLEFEUILLES)

Puff Paste Recipe   *Confectioners' sugar*
Crème Pâtissière Recipe

Divide the pastry into thirds. Roll out ¼ inch thick and cut into 3-inch wide strips. Place on baking sheets and prick the surface of the pastry. Bake in a preheated 375° oven 40 minutes. Cool on a cake rack. Put the layers together with the pastry cream between, or you may use sweetened whipped cream and strawberries. Dust top with confectioners' sugar. Cut in 2-inch slices, using great care.
Serves 10–12.
Note: The dough may be cut into individual serving-sized pieces before baking, if you prefer. Bake 20 minutes or until browned.

PEACH TURNOVER

2 *pounds peaches*   1 *teaspoon vanilla*
3 *tablespoons butter*   ½ *teaspoon almond extract*
¼ *cup sugar*   1 *recipe Puff Paste*
1 *tablespoon cognac*   1 *egg, beaten*

Peel and slice the peaches. Melt the butter in a saucepan. Add the peaches and sugar and cook over low heat 5 minutes,

Pastry / 99

stirring frequently. Add the cognac, vanilla and almond extract. Taste for sweetening—if too tart, add a little sugar. Cool. Preheat the oven to 425°.

Roll out the puff paste into a 12-inch circle ¼ inch thick. Place the peaches in the center. Fold over the dough, moisten the edges with water and press together. Place on a baking sheet; brush the top with the egg.

Bake 30 minutes or until browned. Serve warm.

CREAM PUFFS

(PÂTÉ À CHOUX)

¼ pound butter
1 cup water
1 teaspoon sugar
⅛ teaspoon salt

1⅛ cups sifted flour
3 eggs
1 egg yolk

Cook the butter, water, sugar and salt in a saucepan until butter melts and is boiling. Add the flour all at once, and cook over very low heat, stirring constantly until mixture forms a ball and leaves the sides of the pan. Remove from the heat and add the eggs and egg yolk, one at a time, beating with a wooden spoon after each addition, until glossy.

For large cream puffs, drop by the tablespoon onto a buttered baking sheet, leaving 1 inch between each. Bake in a preheated 400° oven 10 minutes. Reduce the heat to 300° and bake 25 minutes longer or until browned and no beads of moisture remains. Cool before splitting and filling with ice cream, whipped cream or Crème Pâtissière.

Makes 12–14.

For small cream puffs (profiteroles) drop by the teaspoon onto a buttered baking sheet, leaving ½ inch between each. Bake in a preheated 400° oven 10 minutes; reduce the heat to 300° and bake 15 minutes longer or until browned and free from drops of moisture.

Makes about 36.

For Eclairs, force through a pastry tube with a flat end into strips 4 by 1 inches or shape with 2 spoons. Bake as directed for large cream puffs.

PYRAMID CAKE, FRENCH STYLE

(CROQUEMBOUCHE)

1½ cups water
¼ pound (1 stick) butter
1 cup sifted flour
¼ teaspoon salt
4 eggs
1 cup heavy cream

2 tablespoons confectioners' sugar
3 tablespoons orange liqueur
⅔ cup granulated sugar
⅛ teaspoon cream of tartar
1 cup hot water

Preheat the oven to 400°.

Bring one cup of the water and the butter to a boil in a saucepan. Add the flour and salt all at once. Cook over low heat, stirring with a wooden spoon unitl the mixture forms a ball and leaves the sides of the pan. Remove the pan from the heat. Add the eggs, one at a time, beating very well until the mixture is thick and shiny. Place the batter in rounded teaspoonfuls 1 inch apart on an ungreased cooky sheet. Bake 30 minutes or until crisp and lightly golden. Cook on a cake rack. Make a small hole in the base of each puff. Whip the cream until peaks form, sweeten with the confectioners' sugar and fold in the liqueur. Using a pastry bag and a plain tube, fill the puffs with the whipped cream by inserting the point of the tube into the hole in the base of each, or use a small spoon.

Place the sugar, remaining half cup of water and the cream of tartar in a small skillet. Bring to a boil, stirring constantly. Lower the heat and cook until a light amber color, stirring occasionally. Keep the syrup warm over very low heat while building the pyramid. Roll a cream puff in the warm syrup and set it, top (intact) side facing out, around the outer edge of a 9-inch, flat, round plate. Continue and form a ring around the edge of the plate. Fill in the center with more puffs. Over the spaces between the puffs in the first row, make a slightly smaller circle of dipped puffs. Fill in the center again. Continue until there is a total of five circles. Top with one cream puff.

Add one cup hot water to the syrup left in the skillet. Cook slowly, stirring occasionally, to 232° on a candy thermometer. Cool the syrup to room temperature and drizzle it down the sides of the pyramid. Serve the *croquembouche* immediately, from the top, or rifrigerate until needed.

Serves 10–12.

SOUTH AMERICAN COCONUT PASTRIES

(PASTELITOS DE COCO)

2 cups flour
½ teaspoon salt
½ teaspoon baking powder
¼ pound (1 stick) butter
¼ cup orange juice
1½ cups flaked coconut
1 tablespoon cornstarch
½ cup sugar
¾ cup light cream
2 egg yolks
3 tablespoons melted butter, cooled
1 egg white

Sift the flour, salt, and baking powder into a bowl; cut in the butter with a pastry blender or 2 knives until the consistency of coarse cornmeal. Mix in the orange juice until a ball of dough is formed. Chill 1 hour.

Mix together the coconut, cornstarch, sugar, and cream. Cook over low heat, stirring constantly for 5 minutes. Beat the egg yolks and melted butter in a bowl; gradually add the hot mixture stirring constantly. Return to saucepan and stir over low heat for 2 minutes. Cool.

Roll out the dough on a lightly floured surface as thin as possible. Cut into circles with a 3-inch cooky cutter. Place a tablespoon of the coconut mixture on half the circle and cover with the remaining circles. Seal the edges with a little water. Arrange on a baking sheet and brush with the egg white. Bake in a preheated 425° oven 10 minutes, or until delicately browned. Cool on a cake rack.

Makes about 2 dozen.

DANISH PASTRY

Dough

1 package yeast	3 egg yolks, beaten
2 tablespoons sugar	½ teaspoon vanilla extract
¼ cup lukewarm water	½ cup milk, scalded and
2 cups flour	cooled
½ teaspoon salt	½ pound (2 sticks) butter

Dissolve the yeast and sugar in the water. Sift flour and salt into a bowl. Make a well in the center and into it put the yeast mixture, egg yolks, vanilla, milk and 2 tablespoons butter, cut in small pieces. Mix with the fingers until a medium-soft dough is formed, then knead until smooth and elastic. Chill 15 minutes.

Shape the remaining butter into two oblongs, about ¼ inch thick. On a floured surface, roll out the dough into a rectangle about 8 by 20 inches. Place one piece of butter in the center. Fold one long end over the butter and place second piece of butter on top. Fold the other end of dough over it. Press open edges together. Roll out carefully from the short end into a rectangle. Flour the surface again to keep dough from sticking. Brush excess flour from dough and fold long ends over each other. Wrap the dough in waxed paper or foil and chill 30 minutes. Repeat rolling and chilling 3 more times, always rolling from the open ends. Chill 2 hours before final rolling and baking as directed in recipes.

Cheese Filling

¼ pound cream cheese	2 tablespoons sour cream
½ cup cottage cheese,	½ teaspoon vanilla extract
drained	2 tablespoons white raisins
¼ cup sugar	(optional)
1 egg yolk	3 tablespoons heavy cream

Beat all the ingredients together until smooth.

Roll out the Danish Pastry dough ⅛ inch thick. Cut into 4-inch squares. Put a teaspoon of the filling on each. Bring two opposite corners of the dough over the filling and press together firmly. Arrange on greased baking sheets. Chill 20 minutes. Brush with the cream or beaten egg yolk mixed with the cream.

Bake in a preheated 450° oven 10 minutes. Reduce heat to 350° and bake 10 minutes longer or until browned.

Makes about 18.

Prune Filling

1 pound cooked prunes, pitted
½ cup coarsely chopped walnuts or pecans

3 tablespoons melted butter
2 tablespoons grated orange rind
3 tablespoons sugar

Chop the prunes and mix in all the remaining ingredients. Proceed as directed above.

Nut Filling

2 eggs
⅓ cup sugar
⅓ cup melted butter

1½ cups ground almonds, walnuts, pecans or filberts
1 teaspoon vanilla extract

Beat the eggs and sugar until thick and light. Mix in the butter, nuts and vanilla. Proceed as directed above.

Cinnamon Slices

½ cup currants
2 tablespoons cognac
1 egg, beaten
¾ cup sugar

2 teaspoons cinnamon
¾ cup coarsely chopped walnuts

Soak the currants in the cognac 10 minutes. Drain.

Roll out the dough ⅛ inch thick and into a rectangle 5 inches wide by 16 inches long. Brush with the egg, reserving a little. Sprinkle with a mixture of the sugar and cinnamon, then with the currants and nuts. Press the filling down lightly. Roll up like a jelly roll. Seal edges with reserved yolk. Cut into ¾-inch slices. Arrange on a lightly greased baking sheet; flatten slices slightly. Bake as directed.

Makes about 20.

Tarts

FRUIT CREAM TART, PARIS FASHION

3 tablespoons cornstarch
⅛ teaspoon salt
1¼ cups sugar
1 cup light cream
1 cup milk, scalded
3 egg yolks
1 teaspoon vanilla extract

½ cup heavy cream,
　whipped
9-inch baked tart shell
½ cup water
1 teaspoon lemon juice
2 cups sliced peaches,
　blueberries, black cherries
　or halved apricots

In the top of a double boiler, mix the cornstarch, salt and ¼ cup sugar. Mix in the cream, then the hot milk. Place over hot water and cook, stirring steadily until thickened; cook 10 minutes longer, stirring occasionally. Beat the egg yolks in a bowl; gradually add the hot sauce, stirring steadily to prevent curdling. Return to top of double boiler; cook 2 minutes, stirring steadily, but do not let boil. Remove from heat, mix in the vanilla and cool. Fold in the cream and pour into the tart shell. Cook the remaining sugar, the water and lemon juice 5 minutes. Add the selected fruit; cook 5 minutes. Remove the fruit with a slated spoon and cool. Cook the syrup 10 minutes or until very thick. Cool 10 minutes. Arrange the fruit over the cream mixture and brush with the syrup. Cool.

PEACH TART

Pastry for 1-crust pie
1 tablespoon melted butter
3 cups sliced peaches
½ cup sugar

½ teaspoon cinnamon
1 egg yolk
¼ cup heavy cream

Preheat oven to 375°.
Line a 9-inch pie plate with the pastry and brush bottom with the butter. Arrange the peaches in it; sprinkle with the

sugar mixed with the cinnamon. Bake 20 minutes. Beat together the egg yolk and cream; pour over the fruit. Bake 15 minutes longer or until fruit is tender. Cool on a cake rack.

FRENCH LEMON TART

2 eggs
½ cup sugar
⅓ cup lemon juice
¾ cup ground blanched
    almonds

2 teaspoons grated lemon
    rind
¼ teaspoon almond extract
8-inch Tart Pastry-lined pie
    plate, baked 10 minutes
    and cooled

Preheat oven to 325°. Place oven rack on middle level.

Beat the eggs and sugar until very thick and light. Beat in the lemon juice, almonds, lemon rind and almond extract. Turn into the pastry shell. Bake 25 minutes or until a knife inserted in the center comes out clean. Cool on a cake rack.

CHERRY TART, NORMANDY FASHION

1½ pounds black cherries
9-inch unbaked tart shell
½ cup sugar
1 teaspoon lemon juice

⅛ teaspoon almond extract
½ cup currant jelly
2 tablespoons water

Preheat oven to 375°.

Pit the cherries and arrange in the tart shell. Sprinkle with the sugar, lemon juice and almond extract. Bake 30 minutes or until browned and cherries tender. Cool.

Melt the jelly with the water and brush over the cherries until evenly glazed. Cool and decorate with whipped cream, if desired.

INDIVIDUAL FRENCH FRUIT TARTS

(FEUILLETÉS AUX FRUITS DIVERS)

Puff Paste Recipe *Apricots and/or plums*
Egg yolks *Apricot jam*

Make as many or as few tarts as you like. Roll out the pastry ¼-inch thick and fit into tart pans. Brush with the beaten yolks and place a halved apricot or plum, cut side up on each. Bake in a preheated 425° oven 20 minutes or until fruit is tender but firm. Immediately brush with melted apricot jam to glaze fruit.

CARAMELIZED APPLE TART

(TARTE TATIN)

Pastry *3 tablespoons ice water*
1 cup sifted flour **Filling**
⅛ teaspoon salt *6 tablespoons butter*
¼ cup sugar *½ cup sugar*
¼ pound butter *3 cups peeled, sliced apples*

Sift the flour, salt and sugar into a bowl; cut in the butter with a pastry blender or 2 knives. Add the water and toss lightly until a ball of dough is formed. Chill 1 hour.

Use a deep 9-inch pie plate and butter it with 2 tablespoons of the butter. Sprinkle with 3 tablespoons of the sugar. Arrange the apples in layers; dot with the remaining butter and sprinkle with 3 tablespoons sugar. Roll out the pastry and cover the apples with it. Bake in a preheated 375° oven 30 minutes. Cool 5 minutes, then carefully invert onto a serving plate so that the pastry is now underneath, and the apples on top. Sprinkle with the remaining sugar and place under the broiler until sugar browns. Cool.

CHEESE TART

¼ pound (1 stick) sweet
   butter
½ pound cream cheese
⅔ cup sugar
2 eggs

⅛ teaspoon nutmeg
8-inch Tart Pastry-lined pie
   plate, baked 10 minutes
   and cooled

Preheat oven to 375°. Place oven rack on middle level.

Cream the butter with an electric mixer or wooden spoon. Beat in the cheese and sugar until very smooth, then the eggs and nutmeg. Be sure the mixture is smooth and light. Turn into the pastry shell. Bake 25 minutes or until a knife inserted in the center comes out clean. Serve hot, or cool on a cake rack. Don't worry if center sinks slightly.

NUT TART

4 egg yolks
2 cups sugar
2 cups ground toasted
   filberts (hazel nuts)

2 teaspoons vanilla extract
Pastry for 2-crust pie

Preheat the oven to 400°.

Beat the egg yolks, gradually adding the sugar. Beat until thick and smooth. Stir in the nuts and vanilla.

Line a 9-inch pie plate with half the pastry and fill with the nut mixture. Cover with the remaining pastry, sealing the edges well. Bake 35 minutes, or until browned. Cool.

NUT CUSTARD TART

1 cup ground walnuts or
   pecans
9-inch pastry lined pie shell
5 eggs
⅔ cup sugar

2 cups light cream
1 teaspoon vanilla extract
½ cup currant jelly
1 tablespoon cognac

Press nuts into the bottom of the pastry. Chill in the freezing compartment of refrigerator or home freezer 1½ hours.

Beat the eggs and sugar until thick and light. Mix in the cream and vanilla. Pour into the pie shell. Bake in a preheated 350° oven, with rack on lowest rack, 50 minutes or until a knife inserted in the center comes out clean.

While pie is baking, melt the jelly; stir in the cognac. Brush over the top of the pie immediately upon removing from oven. Cool on a cake rack, then chill.

FRENCH ALMOND PASTE TART

(PITHIVIER)

¼ pound butter
½ cup sugar
1 cup blanched ground
  almonds

3 eggs
¼ cup sifted flour
Puff Paste Recipe
1 egg yolk
Confectioners' sugar

Cream the butter, gradually adding the sugar. Beat until creamy and light. Beat in the almonds and 1 egg at a time. Sift in the flour and mix until absorbed.

Roll out the pastry ⅛ inch thick and cut into three 8-inch circles. Brush with beaten egg yolk, then spread the almond mixture on two circles, leaving ½-inch border all around. Put the two together, spread side up and cover with the remaining circle. Press edges together gently. Bake in a preheated 400° oven until browned, about 35 minutes. 5 minutes before baking time is up, sprinkle with confectioners' sugar.

SPANISH ALMOND TARTS

Pastry Shells

2 cups sifted flour
½ teaspoon salt
¼ cup confectioners' sugar

½ pound (2 sticks) butter
1 egg, beaten
¼ cup ice water

Sift the flour, salt ,and sugar into a bowl. Work in the butter with the hand; then blend the egg. Add just enough of the water to make a dough. Chill 2 hours. Roll out ¼ inch thick on a lightly floured surface and fit into twelve tart or muffin tins. Reserve pieces of pastry for tops. Preheat the oven to 425°.

Filling

¼ *pound (1 stick) butter*	*1 cup ground almonds*
½ *cup sugar*	*2 tablespoons cognac*
4 eggs	*1 teaspoon almond extract*

Cream the butter and sugar until fluffy. Beat in the eggs; then stir in the almonds, cognac, and almond extract. Spoon into the pastry shells. Roll out the remaining pastry very thin and cut into narrow strips. Place over the filling in a crisscross fashion. Bake 20 minutes, or until browned and set. Cool and remove from pan.

Serves 12.

Quick Section—Cakes and Pies
Prepared with Mixes

CHOCOLATE PARTY CAKE

1 package chocolate cake
mix

1 package instant chocolate
pudding
¼ cup vegetable oil

Preheat oven to 350°. Grease a 9-inch tube pan and dust lightly with flour.

Prepare cake mix as package directs, but use 2 extra eggs. Add the instant chocolate pudding and oil. Beat with an electric or rotary beater for 2 minutes. Turn into the pan; bake 45 minutes or until a cake tester comes out clean. Cool on a cake rack 10 minutes before removing cake from pan. Finish cooling on the cake rack. The cake may be split and filled and covered with any frosting or whipped cream, or served plain.

APPLESAUCE CAKE

1 package butterscotch cake
mix
½ cup canned applesauce

½ cup chopped walnuts or
pecans
½ teaspoon cinnamon
¼ teaspoon nutmeg

Prepare cake mix as package directs, but reduce water to 1 cup. Mix in the applesauce, nuts, cinnamon and nutmeg. Bake in two 9-inch layer cake pans. Cool. Frost with Seven-Minute Frosting or whipped cream.

NUT CAKE

1 package yellow cake mix
¾ cup ground nuts

1 teaspoon vanilla extract

Prepare cake mix as package directs. Stir in the nuts and vanilla. Bake in two 9-inch layer cake pans. Cool. Frost with Butter Cream Frosting and decorate with nut halves of the variety used in the cake.

COCONUT CAKE

1 package white cake mix
1½ cups fine grated
    coconut

½ teaspoon vanilla extract
1½ cups heavy cream
2 tablespoons sugar

Prepare cake mix as package directs, but fold in ¾ cup coconut and the vanilla. Bake in two 8-inch layer cake pans. Cool. Whip the cream and sugar. Spread some between the layers and sprinkle with ½ cup coconut. Cover cake with whipped cream and sprinkle with the remaining coconut. Chill 1 hour.

LEMON-COGNAC CAKE

1 package lemon custard
    angel food cake mix
1 cup heavy cream

2 tablespoons confectioners'
    sugar
¼ cup cognac
¼ cup candied cherries

Prepare and bake cake mix in a 10-inch tube pan as package directs. Cool on a cake rack 15 minutes, then remove from pan. Finish cooling on the rack.

Whip the cream and sugar, then fold in the cognac. Cover the cake with it and decorate with the cherries.

SPICE LOG

1 package spice cake mix
½ cup confectioners' sugar
1 cup heavy cream,
    whipped

Butter Cream Frosting
Shaved sweet chocolate

Preheat oven to 350°. Oil an 11-by-16-inch jelly roll pan, line it with waxed paper, leaving a 2-inch piece extending at each end, and grease the paper.

Prepare the cake mix as package directs. Pour three-quarters of the mixture into the lined pan and spread it evenly. (Bake excess batter in a small pan or make cupcakes.) Bake 20 minutes.

Sprinkle the confectioners' sugar on a large piece of waxed paper. Turn cake out onto it. Carefully peel off the paper in which the cake was baked. Roll up the cake lengthwise. Cool 1 hour. Unroll cake and spread with the whipped cream. Re-roll cake and cover with the butter cream. Draw a fork over the frosting to mark it like bark. Sprinkle with the chocolate. Chill.

NUN'S TORTE

1 package yellow cake mix
2 egg whites
⅓ cup sugar

¾ cup sliced blanched almonds
1 cup heavy cream

Preheat oven to 350°.

Prepare the cake mix as package directs. Divide batter between two 9-inch layer cake pans. Beat the egg whites until soft peaks are formed, then gradually beat in the sugar until stiff. Spread over the batter to within ½-inch of the outside edge. Sprinkle meringue with the almonds. Bake 40 minutes or until delicately browned and cake shrunk away from the sides of the pans. Cool on a cake rack 30 minutes, then turn out meringue-side up. Cool 2 hours longer.

Whip the cream and spread over one layer. Cover with the remaining layer, meringue-side up.

COCOA SURPRISE CAKE

1 package devil's food cake mix
2 cups heavy cream

¼ cup sugar
⅛ teaspoon salt
¼ cup unsweetened cocoa

Prepare and bake mix as package directs, in a 9-inch square pan. Cool. Cut a 1-inch piece, horizontally, off the top. Carefully hollow out the inside. Combine the cream, sugar, salt and cocoa; chill 1 hour, then whip. Fill the hollow with half the cream, replace top and cover the remaining cream. Chill before serving.

PECAN CUSTARD PIE

Pastry for 1-crust pie
1 cup dark corn syrup
1 package vanilla instant
 pudding
¾ cup light cream
1 egg, beaten
1 cup chopped pecans

Preheat oven to 325°. Line a 9-inch pie plate with the pastry.
Gradually stir the corn syrup into the pudding mix, then add the cream and egg. Mix until smooth. Stir in the pecans. Turn into the lined pie plate. Bake 50 minutes or until a cake tester comes out clean.

REFRIGERATOR LEMON CHEESE PIE

½ pound cream cheese
2 cups sour cream
1 package instant lemon
 pudding
1 teaspoon vanilla extract
1 chilled 9-inch Graham
 Cracker Shell

Beat the cheese until soft, then gradually mix in half the sour cream. Add the pudding mix, vanilla and remaining sour cream, beating with an electric mixer or rotary beater until very smooth and fluffy. Turn into the lined pie plate. Chill until set, about 2 hours.

Frostings, Creams, Glazes and Fillings

SEVEN-MINUTE FROSTING

2 egg whites
⅛ teaspoon salt
1½ cups sugar
½ cup cold water

1 tablespoon light corn
  syrup
1½ teaspoon vanilla extract

In the top of a double boiler, combine the egg whites, salt, sugar, water and corn syrup. Place over boiling water. Beat with an electric mixer or rotary beater 7 minutes, or until stiff peaks form. Turn into a bowl and beat in the vanilla for 1 minute or until thick enough to spread.

Makes about 5½ cups; enough for two layers, a 9-inch square cake or 2 dozen cupcakes.

Variations

Coffee: Add 1 tablespoon instant coffee to unbeaten mixture. Proceed as directed.

Chocolate: Add 2 tablespoons unsweetened cocoa to unbeaten mixture. Proceed as directed.

Cherry: Add 3 tablespoons maraschino cherry juice to unbeaten mixture. Proceed as directed.

Orange: Substitute 2 teaspoons orange extract for the vanilla. Add 1 tablespoon grated orange rind.

Lemon: Substitute 2 teaspoons lemon extract for the vanilla. Add 2 teaspoons grated lemon rind.

Brown Sugar: Substitute 1½ cups firmly packed brown sugar for the granulated sugar. Proceed as directed.

RICH CHOCOLATE FROSTING

5 squares (ounces)
  unsweetened chocolate
2¼ cups sifted
  confectioners' sugar

¼ cup hot light cream
1 egg
6 tablespoons soft butter

114

Break up the chocolate and melt it over hot water. Beat in the confectioners' sugar and cream. Add the egg, beating until smooth and shiny. Add 1 tablespoon butter at a time, beating after each addition, until absorbed.

Makes about 2 cups, enough for two layers, a 9-inch square cake or 18 cupcakes.

BUTTER CREAM FROSTING

¼ pound (1 stick) butter	⅛ teaspoon salt
4 cups sifted confectioners' sugar	1 teaspoon vanilla extract
	2 tablespoons light cream
1 egg	

Cream the butter until soft and fluffy; add half the confectioners' sugar very gradually, beating well after each addition. Blend in the egg, salt and vanilla. Add the remaining sugar alternately with the cream, beating until smooth after each addition. It may not be necessary to add all the sugar to obtain the right consistancy for spreading.

Makes about 2½ cups, enough for two layers, two 9-inch square cakes or 36 cupcakes.

Variations

Coffee Butter Cream: Add 1 tablespoon instant coffee when adding the egg.

Chocolatte Butter Cream: Add 3 squares melted unsweetened chocolate with the first addition of sugar. Increase cream to 4 tablespoons.

Orange Butter Cream: Substitute 2 tablespoons orange juice for the cream, omit vanilla and add 1 tablespoon finely grated orange rind.

CHOCOLATE CREAM CHEESE FROSTING

½ pound sweet chocolate	2 tablespoons light cream
¼ teaspoon salt	2 cups sifted confectioners' sugar
2 3-ounce packages cream cheese	1 teaspoon vanilla extract

Break the chocolate into small pieces and add the salt. Place over hot water until melted. Cool 10 minutes, then beat in the cream cheese and cream. Gradually beat in the confectioners' sugar, then the vanilla.

Makes about 2 cups, enough for two layers, a 9-inch square cake or 24 cupcakes.

CREAM FROSTING

4 cups sifted confectioners' sugar
½ cup melted butter

1 teaspoon vanilla extract
1½ cups heavy cream

Mix the confectioners' sugar, butter and vanilla together. Gradually mix in just enough of the cream to make a spreadable mixture. It may not be necessary to add all the cream.

Enough for three 8-inch layers, two 9-inch layers or two 8-inch square cakes.

PASTRY CREAM

(CRÈME PÂTISSIÈRE)

½ cup flour
1 tablespoon cornstarch
¾ cup sugar

6 egg yolks, beaten
3 cups milk, scalded
1 teaspoon vanilla extract

Sift the flour, cornstarch and sugar into a saucepan. Stir in the egg yolks until smooth. Gradually add the hot milk, stirring steadily to prevent curdling. Cook over low heat, mixing steadily, until thickened. Cool. For a richer cream, 1 cup whipped cream can be folded in. Use for filling cream puffs or napoleons.

CHOCOLATE WHIPPED CREAM

1 cup heavy cream
1 tablespoon sugar

2 tablespoons sifted unsweetened cocoa

Whip the cream until it begins to thicken, then beat in the sugar and cocoa until whipped.

Makes 2 cups.

COFFEE WHIPPED CREAM

2 cups (one pint) heavy
cream

1 tablespoon instant coffee
¼ cup confectioners' sugar

Place cream in a chilled bowl. Beat until cream begins to thicken. Gradually sprinkle in coffee and sugar, continuing to beat until cream is stiff.

CHOCOLATE GLAZE

¼ pound sweet chocolate
3 tablespoons water
1 tablespoon butter

1 cup sifted confectioners'
sugar
⅛ teaspoon salt
¾ teaspoon vanilla extract

Break the chocolate into small pieces; combine in a saucepan with the water and butter. Cook over very low heat until melted and smooth. Sift the confectioners' sugar and salt into a bowl, gradually mix in the melted chocolate. Stir in the vanilla. Cool until thick enough to spread.

Makes about ¾ cup, enough for the top of a 10-inch tube cake or a layer cake.

MOCHA GLAZE

2 tablespoons unsweetened
cocoa
1 teaspoon instant coffee
3 tablespoons hot water

2 tablespoons soft butter
1½ cups sifted
confectioners' sugar

Mix together the cocoa, coffee, water and butter until smooth. Gradually beat in the confectioners' sugar until smooth and spreadable.

Makes enough for the top of a layer cake, an 8-inch square cake, 3 dozen cookies or 2 dozen cupcakes.

APRICOT GLAZE

1 cup apricot preserves

2 tablespoons cognac or fruit liqueur

Makes 1 cup.
Force the preserves through a sieve into a saucepan. Bring to a boil and stir in the liqueur. Use while warm.

ORANGE GLAZE

1 tablespoon butter
1 tablespoon milk
1¼ cups sifted confectioners' sugar

1½ tablespoons orange juice
2 teaspoons grated orange rind

Heat the butter and milk together until butter melts. Stir in the sugar until smooth. Beat in the orange juice and rind. Cool until thick enough to spread.
Makes about ⅔ cup, enough to glaze the top of a 10-inch tube cake or layer cake.

Variation

Lemon Glaze: Substitute lemon juice and rind for the orange juice and rind.

WALNUT BUTTER CREAM FILLING

1¼ cups ground walnuts
2 tablespoons cognac
1 egg white

4 tablespoons sugar
¾ cup (1½ sticks) softened butter

Mix the walnuts and cognac. Combine the egg white and sugar in the top of a double boiler; place over hot water and beat until the consistency of heavy cream. Mix in the walnuts and then gradually beat in the butter. Spread between cake layers or use as a filling for a cake roll.

ORANGE CREAM FILLING

2 tablespoons cornstarch
¾ cup sugar
2 egg yolks, lightly beaten
1 egg white, lightly beaten

⅔ cup orange juice
1 tablespoon butter
2 teaspoons grated orange rind

Mix together all the ingredients but the orange rind in a saucepan. Cook over low heat, stirring constantly until thickened, about 5 minutes. Remove from heat and mix in the orange rind. Cool.

Makes about 1¼ cups, enough to fill two layers.

Variation

Lemon Cream Filling: Substitute 3 tablespoons lemon juice and ½ cup water for the orange juice, and 1 teaspoon grated lemon rind for the orange rind.

Conversion Chart

for Weights, Measures, and Temperature

WEIGHT EQUIVALENTS

American & British	French
1 oz.	30 grams
2 oz.	60 grams
8 oz.	240 grams
1 pound	480 grams

LIQUID EQUIVALENTS

American		British		French
¼ cup	=	2 ounces	=	0.56 deciliters
⅓ cup	=	2½ ounces	=	0.75 deciliters
½ cup	=	4 ounces	=	1.13 deciliters
⅔ cup	=	5 ounces	=	1.5 deciliters
¾ cup	=	6 ounces	=	1.68 deciliters
1 cup	=	8 ounces	=	2.27 deciliters
2 cups	=	16 ounces	=	4.5 deciliters
1 quart	=	32 ounces	=	9 deciliters

OTHER EQUIVALENTS

American & British	French
1 pinch	1 pincée
1 teaspoon	1 cuillère à café
1 tablespoon	1 cuillère à soupe

TEMPERATURE EQUIVALENTS

American (Fahrenheit)	British (Regular)—Fahrenheit	French (Centigrade)
225°	# ¾	Doux 107
250°		
275°	# ½	
300°	#1 (291°)	Moyen 140
325°	#2 (313°)	
350°	#3 (336°)	Assez Chaud 177
	#4 (358°)	
375°	#5 (379°)	
400°	#6 (403°)	
425°	#7 (424°)	Chaud 210
450°	#8 (446°)	
475°	#9 (469°)	Très Chaud 246

Index

Baker, how to become good, 8-11
Baking ingredients, 13-15
Baking terms, definition of, 11-13

Cake failure, how to check, 15-16
Cakes
Baba au Rhum, 45
Brazilian Chocolate-Nut cake, 24
Brazilian Nut Cake, 23
Butter Spongecake, 28
Cake Roll, 30
Cheesecake with Sour Cream, 20
Chocolate Chiffon Cake, 19
Chocolate Roll (Biscuit Roulé au Chocolat), 31
Cocoa Layer Cake, 35
Coconut Cheese Cake, 21
Coffee Cake Wreath, 48
Coffee Crumb Cake, 48
Colombian Cocoa Roll, 31
Cupcakes, 44
Custard-Filled Sponge Roll, 29
Danish Chocolate Yeast Cake, 17
Devil's Food Cupcakes, 45
Dundee Cake, 40
Egg Yolk Cake, 37
English Seed Cake, 41
Fudge Cake, 20
Génoise, 33
Génoise, Chocolate, 33
Génoise, Nut, 33
Hot Milk Spongecake, 27
Italian Spice-Nut Cake (Certosina), 23
Lemon Syrup Cake, 37
Light Fruit Cake, 43
Marquis Chocolate Spongecake, 27
Nut Roll, 32
Orange Cake, 41
Orange Spongecake, 25
Pineapple Upside-Down Cake, 34
Pound Cake, 42
Raisin-Filled Cake, 38
Raisin Tea Cake, 39

Refrigerator Cheese Cake, 22
Refrigerator Coffee Cake Dough, 47
Rich Chocolate Cake, Argentine Style, 17
Savarin, 46
Schnecken, 47
Spanish Tea Cake, 40
Spice-Sour Cream Cake, 22
Spongecake, 25, 28
Tube Cake, 33
Unbaked (Frozen) Fruitcake, 44
Upside-down Chocolate Cake, 19
Viennese Chocolate Layer Cake, 17
Virginia Pound Cake, 42
White Butter Cake, 36
White Cake, 36
Yellow Cake, 35
Cinnamon Slices, 103
Conversion Chart, 121-22
Cookies
Almond Cookies, 60
Almond Meringue Strips, 65
Austrian Nut Crescents, 67
Barcelona Almond Drops (Roscas Almendra), 65
Chocolate Nut Drop Cookies, 68
Cream Cheese Cookies, 58
Crisp Butter Cookies, 61
Crisp Chocolate Nut Cookies, 67
Crisp Sugar Cookies, 59
English Molasses Drop Cookies, 58
Italian Crullers (Sfinge), 77
Jam Cookies, 62
Meringue Coconut Cookies, 63
Molasses Nut Cookies, 59
Molasses Raisin Cookies, 59
Nut Slices, 66
Oatmeal Cookies, 61
Spanish Almond Delights, 64
Swedish Honey Cookies, 62
Vienna Sugar Cookies (Sablé Viennois), 60

Viennese Almond Crescents, 66
Walnut Slices, 64

Frostings, Creams, Glazes and Fillings
Apple Filling, 96
Apricot Glaze, 26, 118
Brown Sugar Frosting, 114
Butter Cream Frosting, 115
Cheese Filling, 96, 102
Cherry Frosting, 114
Chocolate Butter Cream, 115
Chocolate Cream Cheese Frosting, 115-16
Chocolate Frosting, 17, 35, 45, 114
Chocolate Glaze, 27, 117
Chocolate Whipped Cream, 50, 116-17
Coffee Butter Cream, 115
Coffee Frosting, 114
Coffee Whipped Cream, 18, 117
Cream Frosting, 116
Custard Filling, 29
Frosting, 52
Lemon Cream Filling, 119
Lemon Frosting, 114
Lemon Glaze, 118
Mint Frosting, 35
Mocha Glaze, 68, 117-18
Nut Filling, 103
Orange Butter Cream, 115
Orange Butter Frosting, 41
Orange Cream Filling, 26, 119
Orange Frosting, 114
Orange Glaze, 118
Pastry Cream (Crème Pâtissière), 116
Poppy Seed Filling, 97
Prune Filling, 103
Rich Chocolate Frosting, 114
Seven-Minute Frosting, 35, 114
Walnut Butter Cream Filling, 118-19
White Frosting, 45

Liquid Equivalents, 121

Macaroons
Butterscotch Brownies, 72-73
Butterscotch Squares, 73
Chocolate-Almond Macaroons, 69
Chocolate Balls, 74
Chocolate Date-Nut Bars, 74
Coconut Macaroons, 69
Coconut Pecan Squares, 73
Coconut Shortbread, 76
Dutch Poppy Seed Bars, 75
Florentines, 70
Fudge Brownies, 72
Gingersnaps, 71
Israeli Almond Macaroons, 69
Ladyfingers, 71
Peppermint Brownies, 72
Polish Almond Bars (Mazurka), 75
Scotch Shortbread, 76
Spanish Crisps, 70
Meringue, 50
Mixes
Applesauce Cake, 110
Chocolate Party Cake, 110
Cocoa Surprise Cake, 112-13
Coconut Cake, 111
Lemon-Cognac Cake, 111
Nun's Torte, 112
Nut Cake, 110-11
Pecan Custard Pie, 113
Refrigerator Lemon Cheese Pie, 113
Spice Log, 111-12

Pastry
Cheese Pastry, 91
Chocolate Crumb Pastry Shell, 95
Coconut Meringue Shell, 94
Cream Puffs (Pâté à Choux), 99
Danish Pastry, 102
Flaky Pastry, 92
French Puff Paste (Pâté Feuilletée), 97-98
French Tart Paste (Pâté Sucrié), 91
Gingersnap Crumb Pastry Shell, 95
Graham Cracker Pastry Shell, 94
Hungarian Strudel, 95
Meringue Pastry Shell, Paris Style, 94
Napoleons (Millefeuillis), 98
Pyramid Cake, French Style (Croquembouche), 100
Sour Cream Pastry, 92
South American Coconut Pastries (Pastelitos de Coco), 101

Walnut Pastry, 93
Zwieback Pastry Shell, 95
Pastry Shells, 108
Pies
Apple Pie, 79
Apple-Cheese Pie, 80
Apple Custard Pie, 80
Banana Pie, 82
Berry Pie, 78
Black Bottom Pie, 88
Black Walnut Pie, 88
Blueberry Pie, 78
Boston Cream Pie, 85
Canned Red Cherry Pie, 78
Cheese Pie, 89
Chocolate Cream Pie, 90-91
Coconut Custard Pie, 80
Coconut Meringue-Shell Pie, 91
Crustless Fudge Pie, 90
Fresh Red Cherry Pie, 79
Fruit Custard-Meringue Pie, 81
Italian Fruit-Almond Pie, 84
Lemon Chiffon Pie, 83
Lemon-Curd Meringue Pie, 82
Lemon Sponge Pie, 83
Lime Chiffon Pie, 84
Mocha Chiffon Pie, 84
Orange-Custard Pie, 81
Pecan Pie, 89
Pumpkin Pie, 87
Sweet Potato-Nut Pie, 91
Vanilla Cream Pie, 90

Rum Syrup, 46

Tarts

Caramelized Apple Tart (Tarte Tatin), 106
Cheese Tarts, 107

Cherry Tart, Normandy Fashion, 105
French Almond Paste Tart (Pithivier), 108
French Lemon Tart, 105
Fruit Cream Tart, Paris Fashion, 104
Individual French Fruit Tarts (Feuilletés aux Fruits Divers), 106
Nut Custard Tart, 107-8
Nut Tart, 107
Peach Tart, 104
Spanish Almond Tarts, 108-9
Temperature Equivalents, 122
Thoughts about making cakes, cookies and pastry 7-15
Tortes
Apricot Meringue Torte, 50
Austrian Chocolate Torte, 49
Austrian Filbert Torte, 54
Austrian Linzer (Almond) Torte, 55
Carrot Torte, 56
Italian Chestnut Refrigerator Torte (Gato de Castagne), 53
Italian Chestnut Torte (Torta de Castagne), 52
Italian Rum Torte (Zuppa Inglese), 56
Swiss Almond Torte, 55
Swiss Torte, 53
Venezuelan Banana Torte, 51
Viennese Cocoa Torte, 49-50
Viennese Poppy Seed Torte, 51

Variations in cake recipe, 7

Weight Equivalents, 121